Cultural History

The expression 'cultural history' is generally used today to signal a particular approach to history, one which could be applied to any object, and is mainly concerned with the sense men and women from the past gave to the world they lived in.

In this introduction to cultural history as a subdiscipline, the reader will find the key steps in the historical development of the field from 1850 to the present. It surveys different ways in which cultural history has been practised, exploring intellectual history, the history of ideas and concepts, of mentalities, of symbols and representations, and of languages and discourses.

Cultural History also maps the territory cultural history most effectively enlightens: gender; the family and sexuality; the body; senses and emotions and images; material culture and consumption; the media and communication. Lastly, it includes an appendix of biographies of a number of influential cultural historians.

This concise and accessible introduction will be an essential volume for any university student studying cultural history.

Alessandro Arcangeli is Associate Professor of Early Modern History at the University of Verona, Italy. He has studied the cultural history of Renaissance Europe, with particular focus on dance (*Davide o Salomè?*, 2000), leisure (*Recreation in the Renaissance*, 2003) and the medical discourse on lifestyle.

Cultural History

A Concise Introduction

Alessandro Arcangeli

LONDON AND NEW YORK

First published 2012
by Routledge
2 Park Square, Milton Park, Abingdon, Oxon OX14 4RN

Simultaneously published in the USA and Canada
by Routledge
711 Third Avenue, New York, NY 10017

Routledge is an imprint of the Taylor & Francis Group, an informa business

British Library Cataloguing in Publication Data
A catalogue record for this book is available from the British Library

Library of Congress Cataloging in Publication Data
Arcangeli, Alessandro.
  [Che cos'è la storia culturale. English]
  Cultural history : a concise introduction / Alessandro Arcangeli.
    p. cm.
  "Simultaneously published in the USA and Canada"–T.p. verso.
  Includes bibliographical references and index.
  1. Civilization–History. 2. Culture–History. 3. Intellectual life–History. 4. Social history. I. Title.
  CB151.A7613 2012
  306.09–dc22
        2011015445

ISBN: 978-0-415-66775-3 (hbk)
ISBN: 978-0-415-66776-0 (pbk)
ISBN: 978-0-203-78924-7 (ebk)

Typeset in Times New Roman
by Taylor & Francis Books

MIX
Paper from
responsible sources
FSC
www.fsc.org   FSC® C004839

Printed and bound in Great Britain by the MPG Books Group

To my father and in memory of my mother

Contents

Preface

Cultural history is developing quickly as one of the most dynamic subfields or ways of doing history. It is the subject of an increasing volume of publications. A number of academic institutions have begun to acknowledge this fairly recent trend: in various countries it is now taught as the subject of specific courses, if not of entire degrees; national and international associations have taken it as their dedicated area of work. Among the latter, the International Society for Cultural History (ISCH) deserves mention (www.abdn.ac.uk/isch). The Society was planned at a conference held in 2007 at the University of Aberdeen, Scotland, UK (where an MA in Cultural History was taught from 1986 to 2011), and launched at a subsequent conference the following year in Ghent. Yearly ISCH conferences followed in Brisbane, Turku and Oslo, as well as other initiatives run by the Society, which include (to date, plans for) a *Journal of Cultural History*.

This book was originally written in Italian and conceived for an Italian audience. The editorial staff at Routledge and their advisors considered that it would be worth re-presenting to a worldwide, English-speaking audience. In rewriting it, in consideration of changes in the editorial context and expected uses of my text, I have slightly adapted, updated and developed it; however, in essence, it remains the same book. In a volume inevitably full of names, an Appendix of sixty-four short biographies has been added to provide a quick guide to the key authors mentioned. It goes without saying that this is no substitute for – on the contrary, it is meant as an incentive and aid to – further reading of material on and by the historians and theorists listed. On first mention in the book, the surnames of authors who have a biography appear in bold.

The first chapter introduces working definitions of culture and cultural history, and sets the field in its relationship with social history and social theory. The second offers a selective survey of significant figures and ways of doing cultural history from the mid-nineteenth century onwards. The third examines a variety of (partly competing) approaches and paradigms of cultural historical research. The fourth, last and broadest chapter reconsiders the areas such trends in historical writing have investigated, their sources, and their most representative topics and findings. Each chapter ends with a short summary to assist in identifying and memorizing its main points. The suggestions included in the section on further reading are deliberately limited to examples of books *on*, rather than *of*, cultural history. My bibliography, text and the books recommended there contain abundant references to the latter.

Acknowledgements

Federico Barbierato, Peter Burke, Alex Drace-Francis, Anne Eriksen, Cecilia Miller, Ottavia Niccoli, Steven Schouten and Patrizia Veroli are among the friends and colleagues who provided me with helpful encouragement and recommendations at one or more stages of preparation of either the original edition or the present version of this book, or both. I would like to thank them all dearly. My grateful thanks also go to the editorial staff in history at Routledge – in particular to Eve Setch and Laura Mothersole – who believed in this project promptly, with conviction and determination.

1 In search of a definition
A fuzzy field of enquiry

As a field of historical enquiry, cultural history has recently witnessed major developments. Over the past few years, many books have been published that purport, in their title or subtitle, to be the cultural history of one or another among a disparate assortment of entities and phenomena: just to mention a few, an internet search with the appropriate key words in some European languages produced topics ranging from the cultural history of individual countries or communities, or even rivers and valleys (the Amazon River, the Grand Canyon), to that of the body, of sport, fashion, cinema, pregnancy, suicide or the punch card. A similar search on book catalogues can easily fill a page with topics that have been explored from this perspective (Serna and Pons 2005: 15–16). To the difference that distances these objects from one another, and its implications for a definition of the field, I will return later. Their diversity recalls the exotic incongruity of 'a certain Chinese encyclopaedia', a product of the narrative invention of Argentinean writer Jorge Luis Borges, from whom **Michel Foucault** (2002: xvi) borrowed it within the preface of one of his first works, to epitomize the variability of systems of thought: the extreme diversity of the criteria according to which it classifies the animal world provokes the reader's laughter.

In passing, it is worth pointing out that there is a clearly perceivable risk that time will reveal the cultural history boom to have been little more than a fad; or that this field may be exercising, on neighbouring disciplines, the kind of imperialism that not long ago was exercised in cultural studies by other approaches (such was arguably, between the 1970s and the 1980s, the role of semiotics). On the other hand, the area is also characterized to some extent by elusiveness. Although cultural history is gaining credibility and institutionalization, this is not yet true everywhere. In a significant number of countries, it is not an academic discipline or the object of specific teaching; and, as a type of approach to the past, it has often shown the tendency to be associated with amateur history publications for a non-specialist audience, rather than the work of professional historians. The latter association has occurred before in the not-so-distant past, and for this reason we will revisit it in Chapter 2.

As for the identity of this field of knowledge, introductions to cultural history recently published in various languages (see Suggestions for further reading), as well as entries in reference books that deal with the subject, have adopted a heterogeneous series of positions. They range from the statement that it is a field easy to define, to the refusal to provide any delimitation; from the hypothesis that what characterizes it is a particular object (as distinguished from that peculiar to other historical subdisciplines), to the adoption of a specific method. In what follows, the reader will find no demand for regulation. The present writer has no intention of establishing how historians should get on with their job, nor of erecting fencing to define who is in and who out (it is likely that both the excluded and the unwillingly included would have something to object about). It will be, rather, a question of registering how this area has acquired its shape, in the eyes of both the scholars and authors who are its practitioners, and the readers and reviewers of other people's writing. To be more accurate – and this should be said once and for all – rather than a single, welldefined field, what we intend to explore is a series of parallel, sometimes crossing and overlapping research paths. However, this lack of uniformity should not necessarily be perceived as a limit. Somehow, the 'weak' character of this area bears the inevitable imprint of the postmodern condition (Lyotard 1984), to which several threads link it. What in other times and by different judges might have been stigmatized as a sign of instability or an unsafe methodological foundation, one can reasonably value today as an endowment and as evidence of an experimental spirit. As we shall soon see, this complexity of definition is largely the result of a shift that has occurred in this area of study. As a first approximation, we could describe it as a gradual transition (one that occurred over generations of historians, during the past 150 years) from a 'history of culture' defined as a specific field (culture as the object of enquiry) to a 'cultural history' characterized by the ways it approaches the subject (regardless of the variety of its themes).

Cultures and history

So, to begin with, the difference between the phrases 'history of culture' and 'cultural history' should be clarified. In the former, the genitive case delimits an *object* of enquiry (culture rather than politics, the economy or something else); in the latter, the adjective qualifies one of the available ways at our disposal for examining any historical objects (topics, events, circumstances). In this respect, it differs from other approaches (in particular, the cultural perspective has constantly competed or been woven together with the social one, as we shall soon see); on the other hand, it does not have precise limits on the fields to which it applies (potentially, history as a whole, as well as each of its individual moments). In principle, this is a valid distinction, and, as a rule, it will be used in this book. Nevertheless, it does incur problems, and is not universally accepted. There is no agreement among scholars upon the definition of the discipline and of its distinctive features; the rise of cultural history from the history of culture is itself a historical phenomenon (we will examine it in Chapter 2); and, in some linguistic domains, historiography seems to have resisted the introduction of the adjectival form ('cultural', rather than 'of culture'). Sometimes – particularly in the past – this resistance has taken the form of adapted translations, which persisted in using the old expression even when presenting new foreign research to national audiences.

If one considers how the expression appears in different languages, in fact, the situation varies considerably and becomes more complex. Historically, the mother of all these words is German *Kulturgeschichte*. Grammatically, it is a compound name. The main term is history (*Geschichte*); *Kultur* is in attributive position (German tends to combine words, while English keeps them separate). If we check the meaning of *Kultur* in the Germanic tradition, however, we knock against a term of extreme complexity and historical relevance. A wellknown and meaningful page of the story may cast sufficient light on some of its implications. At the outbreak of World War I, Thomas Mann and other intellectuals interpreted what was happening as a clash of civilizations: on one side Germanic *Kultur*, which had produced unparalleled masterpieces in music and literature, and also the deepest chapters in recent Western philosophy and, with them, a rigorous moral law, a bulwark defending a really valuable way of life; on the other side, Anglo-French *Zivilization*, which was utilitarian and superficial, governed as it was – in the view of the German intellectuals – by the value systems of money and fashion. Although this particular representation of cultural differences was shaped by nationalism and other contextual elements, the case provides a telling example of the importance of the issue, charged as it was with strong identity markers (Bénéton 1975). If we consider the etymological proximity between *Zivilization* and the English 'civilization' (and related words in other languages), it is therefore a paradox that it is precisely 'civilization' that is commonly regarded as the closest and most appropriate equivalent for German *Kultur*. Classic works by the Swiss historian **Jacob Burckhardt** can provide a good example: his essay *Die Kultur der Renaissance in Italien* is in fact translated as *The Civilization of the Renaissance in Italy* (Burckhardt 1990).[1]

This considered, where have we got to from our starting point? In Chapter 2 we will examine the characteristics of the nineteenth-century German historiography that first delimited and ploughed through this field of enquiry. However, it can be stated already that German *Kulturgeschichte* is something more than a history of culture. While it is not simply identifiable with the historiographical traditions typical of different linguistic domains, recent use of the term confirms that it corresponds more closely to an approach that is available to be applied to a wide range of research topics; this is precisely the meaning we have assigned above to the expression 'cultural history'.[2]

The tradition of French terms is as rich in history and connotations. *Civilisation* is a term of eighteenth-century coinage. Outlining its semantic history in an essay originally published in 1930, **Lucien Febvre** – one of the protagonists of the renewal which French historiography experienced between the two World Wars – distinguished between two very different notions, and aimed at narrating the genesis of such a divergence:

> In the first case civilization simply refers to all the features that can be observed in the collective life of one human group, embracing their material, intellectual, moral and political life and, there is unfortunately no other word for it, their social life. It has been suggested that this should be called the 'ethnographical' conception of civilization. It does not imply any value judgment on the detail or the overall pattern of the facts examined. Neither does it have any bearing on the individual in the group taken separately, or on their personal reactions or individual behaviour. It is above all a conception which refers to a group.
>
> In the second case, when we are talking about the progress, failures, greatness and weakness of civilization we do have a value judgment in mind. We have the idea that the civilization we are talking about – ours – is in itself something great and beautiful; something too which is nobler, more comfortable and better, both morally and materially speaking, than anything outside it – savagery, barbarity or semi-civilization. Finally, we are confident that such civilization, in which we participate, which we propagate, benefit from and popularize, bestows on us all a certain value, prestige, and dignity. For it is a collective asset enjoyed by all civilized

societies. It is also an individual privilege which each of us proudly
boasts that he possesses.

(Burke 1973: 220)

Three-quarters of a century later, the least one can say is that pride in that
possession has become feebler, and Febvre's page seems to belong to a
now unrecoverable past, and to exemplify an interpretation of the relationship between cultures now rightly abandoned. An itinerary through
the history of the notions of civility and civilization will be outside our
present agenda. Two or three meaningful passages, however, will prove
relevant to our discourse here. Within the French historical school – the
most influential on the twentieth-century international scene – **Fernand
Braudel**, Febvre's direct heir, is the scholar who, in the second post-war
period, has contributed most substantially to a history of civilization
mainly conceived in terms of *material culture*, collective structures of
economic life centred on market and exchange, and entrenched in
shared rhythms and gesture, repeated for centuries.

From the 1980s, a prominent historical model that has animated
debate on this front is the one revolving around the work of a German
sociologist, **Norbert Elias**, and the relatively slow international reception of his oeuvre. Elias's paradigm (see also Daniel 2001: 254–69) is
that of a 'civilizing process', by which the foundations of our own
present world are understood to have been laid, between the Middle
Ages and the early modern period, via a gradual variation of political
forms, but also in styles of behaviour, and particularly the self-control
of impulses. Several critics have found his model culpable of ethnocentrism, as if, once more, the European pattern were to be proposed
as unparalleled exception, lacking connections with the surrounding
world. From this point of view, the most consistent alternative paradigm is probably offered by Felipe Fernández-Armesto, a Spanish–
British historian who explicitly denies progress or any predictable
direction in history. He has further developed the historical geography
(or geographical history) typical of the French school by exploring, in
essays characterized by boundless geographical and chronological
coordinates, the whole range of human *civilizations*: each of them grew in
relation to given environmental circumstances; none had the monopoly of
putting forward a particular way of life as if universally valid.

Cultures and society

In one sense, it is precisely by distinction from the social approach that
the cultural one defines itself: as we will see in further detail in

Chapter 3, it is specifically a question of focusing on mentalities, representations and discourses rather than contexts, living conditions or movements. In one of the richest and most perceptive overviews of the discipline, Ute Daniel suggested that cultural history

> questions the past by asking how people at the time perceived and interpreted themselves, what material, mental and social motivations respectively influenced their forms of perception and production of sense, and the effects such forms produced.
>
> (Daniel 2001: 19)

Miri Rubin (2002: 81) put it like this: 'Like all good ideas the basic point is simple. The cultural turn asks not only "How it really was" but rather "How was it for him, or her, or them?"' In the course of the twentieth century, stress on one aspect or the other – reality versus representation – also corresponded to shifts in the dominant historiographical paradigms. For instance, a journal in the forefront, such as the French *Annales*, engaged predominantly on a socio-economic front for a long time, despite the fact that its founders had offered crucial contributions to the cultural perspective. With later generations of scholars, however, the same periodical acknowledged and participated in the *cultural turn* in France.

As the two key orientations in recent historiography, social and cultural history have been both complementing and competing with each other. One of the most prominent German social historians, Hans-Ulrich Wehler (2001), has described the confrontation between the two branches of the discipline as a duel; while **Peter Burke** (2008b: 114–18), registering the oscillations in the field from one pole to the other, and reactions to some aspect or excess of the new cultural history, has spoken in terms of a 'revenge of social history'. A return to a kind of history of society after the predominance of the cultural was also called for in an intellectual autobiography by American historian Geoff Eley (2005).

Nevertheless, comparison and mutual reference between the two sides of the coin (reality/representation) are inevitable, and it is precisely in the direction of a socio-cultural perspective that some of the most highly esteemed historians have programmatically moved.

A tradition dating back already a few generations links the combined historical analysis of these two factors to a social and cultural critique of the present state of affairs. *Culture and Society 1780–1950* – written by **Raymond Williams** (1958), the most influential forerunner of modern cultural studies – explicitly inspired Peter Burke (1972), whose first substantial book made use of sociology as a tool to unhinge a sweetened and ahistorical image of the visual and literary civilization of Renaissance Italy. The study was based on close examination of a sample of 'creative elite': a list – given as an appendix of the first edition – of 600 painters and sculptors, writers, musicians, scientists and humanists, 'something like a social survey of the dead' (Burke 1972: 294), in order to study the paths of their careers (recruiting, formation, organization, secular or ecclesiastic condition) and their intersections with social and geographical origins.

Subsequently, the same author re-examined the social dimension of culture in his now classic study of popular culture. When updating that volume and reflecting on the historiographical questions raised by it, he pointed out:

> In the age of the so-called 'discovery' of the people, in the early nineteenth century, the term 'culture' tended to refer to art, literature and music, and it would not be unfair to describe the nineteenth-century folklorists as searching for popular equivalents for classical music, academic art, and so on.
>
> Today, however, following the example of the anthropologists, historians and others use the term 'culture' much more widely, to refer to almost everything that can be learned in a given society – how to eat, drink, walk, talk, be silent and so on. Even kinship is now analysed from a cultural rather than or as well as social point of view. In other words, the history of culture now includes the history of the assumptions underlying everyday life.
>
> (Burke 2009b: 15–16)

In the following chapters we will return to this range of themes and perspectives.

Partition lines and affiliations are neither fixed nor easy to mark. A variety of research paths move simultaneously on different levels, or in territories that defy simple and clear-cut classification. A number of authors, works, topics and research orientations that are discussed in this book, including some of the most prominent figures, as **Carlo Ginzburg**, **Natalie Zemon Davis** and **Robert Darnton**, could be – and have legitimately been – described as representatives of *social* history. This was the headline under which they were labelled at the time of writing of some of their bestknown contributions. In the end, if today there is a tendency to relate them to research developments centred on cultural identities, it is rather due to a shift in the observing point, in other words, to the newly predominant historiographical paradigms.

Anyway, the proximity between the two approaches is such that the two terms are, to some extent, interchangeable. Peter Burke (2008b: 115) has proposed a convincing personal criterion for choosing between them: it is appropriate to speak of *social* history to define a particular approach to facts that are cultural *per se* (such as language), where to specify that they are considered from a cultural perspective would not be very informative; on the other hand, it is worth identifying as *cultural* the way the new history considers phenomena that would appear to be natural (such as landscape or the body; see Chapter 4).

Whatever the label, the trends of research in question here clearly deal with both culture and society, sometimes by advancing original solutions precisely on the interface, or meeting ground, between different planes or aspects of history. By so doing, one can avoid both a narrative of cultural facts oblivious of social stratification and its implications, and a history of material conditions of subsistence of individuals and groups that ignores the world representations appropriated by their protagonists, and the extent to which such representations influence their social agency.

Thus the perspective is somehow inevitably a socio-cultural one – a suggestion also repeatedly put forward by **Roger Chartier**, the French scholar who has most consistently engaged in methodological reflection on this front. It is also what, in a balance sheet of 'the shapes of social history', was claimed at the end of the 1980s by Natalie Zemon Davis (1990). On one side, she saw a more traditional social history, occupied in reconstructing impersonal structures and processes, with strong ties with sociology and economics; on the other side, the more recent cultural orientation, with focus on individuals and small groups, and privileged relationships with anthropology and literature. Between the two directions, the American historian expected and hoped for a good degree of synthesis. An interaction, therefore, has been in place for some time with a variety of disciplines.

Cultural history and cultural anthropology

As a testimony to the aforementioned shift and widening of perspective, it is no surprise that a pioneer of the encounter between history and social sciences such as Peter Burke, who first entitled an essay on the interaction between the two, *Sociology and History*, later enlarged it under the new title *History and Social Theory* (Burke 1980, 2005). There he retraced the itinerary of the relationships between history and social sciences, starting with 'a dialogue of the deaf', to come, after the emergence of social history, to 'the convergence of theory and history'.[3]

The same scholar proposed a similar, partly coinciding scheme for an account of the interaction between history and the specific field of folklore studies – the main difference between the two narratives being that in this case there appears to have been an even longer-lasting 'age of suspicion', replaced only from the 1960s onwards by signs of mutual interest (Burke 2004a).

Twentieth-century French culture was the theatre of explicit confrontations between history and the other human or social sciences on more than one occasion – at the beginning of the century, with the sociology of Émile Durkheim (1858–1917). However, the clash was more complex and cut across disciplines by showing various scholars aligned with different positions, questioning both whether history could legitimately aspire to the status of science, and what particular notion of science was suitable to the specific case of historical knowledge. The foundation by **Marc Bloch** and Lucien Febvre of the *Annales* – the flagship journal of their idea of history – may also be read as the implementation, twenty-five years later, of the model of historical knowledge that had been a programmatic elaboration precisely within those early twentieth-century comparisons with social sciences, on such arenas of debate as the *Revue de Synthèse Historique*, founded by Henri Berr in 1900, and Durkheim's *Année Sociologique* (Burguière 1982, 2009; Burke 1990).

The study of witchcraft subsequently offered a particularly fertile terrain of encounter between history and anthropology. For that purpose, the British historian **Keith Thomas** and his doctoral student Alan Macfarlane (who dealt with the cases that occurred in Essex) made use of a theoretical model elaborated by Edward Evans-Pritchard for a people of central Africa, the Azande. Like Thomas, Evans-Pritchard was active in Oxford, where he taught social anthropology, and from 1950 onwards had expressly advocated a convergence between his discipline and history.

The model of explanation elaborated on that occasion was centred on the hypothesis that, in early modern England, witchcraft accusations were the result of the sense of guilt of men who refused to give charity to elderly women beggars, once cared for by the community, now increasingly replaced by institutionalized welfare. This interpretation of the roots of the witch-hunt would not receive significant confirmations in subsequent research; however, the mere fact that historians regarded it as a phenomenon deserving serious scholarly attention was the sign of a turning point. Over the next few years, as historians and anthropologists took more interest in each other's research tools, a wider variety of topics and ways of conducting research developed which, to some extent, drew the work of the historian near to that of an anthropologist – a significant connotation for the historical profession as it is practised by some of its protagonists.

Microhistory is commonly acknowledged as one such research pattern. A contribution to the new history of the 1970s and 1980s that has also attracted recent critical attention (Bell 2002; Brewer 2010), it was in its origins (see Burke 2008a) an Italian enterprise, although it has been compared methodologically with contemporary work produced elsewhere: for instance, with Natalie Zemon Davis's study of a case of mistaken identity in fifteenth-century France (Davis 1983); or that by Emmanuel Le Roy Ladurie (1978) on the Occitan village of Montaillou at the time of the Albigensian heresy.[4]

Carlo Ginzburg and Giovanni Levi practised microhistory and were its two main theoretical spokespersons. The story of a miller from sixteenth-century Friuli (in north-eastern Italy) who ended up tried by the Inquisition for his heterodox beliefs (Ginzburg 1980) has become so well known today that concerns have been raised that modern students or readers may come to know such improbable hero figures (Ginzburg's Menocchio or Davis's false and true Martin Guerre – both presented to a larger-than-usual audience thanks to cinema or TV broadcasts) better than the protagonists of 'old' history such as Martin Luther or Charles V. In this area of scholarship, the choice of topic was expressly dictated by the will to study common people rather than the powerful; it was also a question of scale, the preference for studying a small community (typically a village) in detail, with all its implications, in the way that anthropologists did. More accurately, considering that small communities do not live in isolation from the context to which they belong, and that history's main issues could also be met, in their local expression, through the microhistorical approach, the question was to study history *in the* village, rather than studying *the* village (Levi 2001, paraphrasing what **Clifford Geertz** had said – the latter, though, about anthropology). The approach brings some problems, since one needs to understand if, and to what extent, the example is typical of a wider phenomenon, and of what exactly; or else, even if we establish that it is relatively atypical, how much it can nevertheless be helpful in shedding light on the community it concerns. All these issues have been widely discussed over the years in the specialized literature devoted to historical method.

Anthropologie historique is a notion that has been regularly used by the French school that we identify with two sister institutions: the periodical *Annales* and the Parisian École des Hautes Études en Sciences Sociales (founded in 1975 from an existing structure, the sixth section of the École Pratique des Hautes Études). Within the latter, the phrase *anthropologie historique* was used as early as 1976 in the title of courses, and has remained since as characteristic of a house style (Valensi and Wachtel 1996). Ten years later, this area of study had developed so much that one of its spokespersons – André Burguière, a specialist in the history of family structures who taught historical anthropology until his recent retirement – found it difficult to draw up a balance sheet, and opted for discussing his topic by subdividing it into a series of distinct subfields in order to give the reader an indication of the main directions of ongoing research. His categories included:

- a *material and biological anthropology*, concerned with the history of the body, of attitudes towards life and sex, or of food habits (see Chapter 4);
- an *economic anthropology*, capable of giving an account of the genesis and transformation of economic attitudes by relating them also to the social, ethical or religious goals that people from the past aimed at obtaining through them;
- a *social anthropology*, paying special attention to demographic factors and to the history of the family and kin, with all their implications and regional variations;
- a *cultural and political anthropology*, interested in the world of popular practice and beliefs, though not neglectful of the connections that cut through the social hierarchy:

> the forms of behaviour less frequently argued within a given society such as body care, dress codes, work structures and the calendar of daily activities reflect a system of world representation that connects them deeply to the most elaborate intellectual statements, such as religious beliefs, law, and philosophical or scientific thought.
>
> (Burguière 1986: 56–57)

According to the same author, the most appropriate expression to define the field of historical anthropology as a whole was 'a history of *behaviour* and *habits* – what in the eighteenth century was known as a history of *customs* [*moeurs*]' (*ibid.*: 54). In the tradition of the *Annales*, focus on uses was deliberately meant to contrast with that on events, the typical concern of history of a more traditional kind: sometimes resorting to stereotype and caricature, the French school tends to represent the latter as solely concerned with politics, battles and diplomacy. Since the 1960s, 'historical anthropology' has been a common expression in Germany too (see Chapter 4). However, in a sense, to be accurate, the phrase would literally appear to signal a particular kind of anthropology (such as, for instance, the use of historical documents by **Marshall Sahlins**), rather than a particular kind of history: thus, in other national contexts, it has been predominantly used by anthropologists.[5]

A scholar who has personally followed these borderline paths between disciplines suggests that what can be more modestly said that historians have intended to do is to draw on the neighbouring discipline for hints and inspiration, rather than full conversion and, as it were, career change; consequently, it would be more fitting to refer to the result of such efforts as 'anthropological history' (Gentilcore 2005).

As mentioned above, the relationships between the two disciplines have nonetheless encountered moments of tension and distinction. Even the groundbreaking study of Thomas (1971), devoted to religion and the decline of magic in sixteenth- and seventeenth-century England, has been met with some resistance among anthropologists, as it made use of categories that were not easily transferable from one culture to another – that is to say, it could be partly charged with anachronism (or displacement, its spatial equivalent). Furthermore, the key representatives of microhistory have criticized the most fashionable anthropological paradigms: for instance, Levi has objected to the way historians such as Robert Darnton use the interpretive anthropology of the American scholar Clifford Geertz.

One of the most influential figures on the international scene in the last quarter of the twentieth century, Geertz is known particularly for having put forward in the early 1960s, above all on the basis of his ethnographical research in Bali, a model of 'thick description' intended to overcome the purely observational aspects of the discipline, and having explicitly taken as a methodological reference point the task of the literary critic. In the opening piece of his bestknown collection of essays, Geertz distanced himself from the fragmentation his teacher Clyde Kluckhohn had imposed on the notion of culture; within a general introduction to anthropology, the latter writer

> managed to define culture in turn as: (1) 'the total way of life of a people'; (2) 'the social legacy the individual acquires from his group'; (3) 'a way of thinking, feeling, and believing'; (4) 'an abstraction from behavior'; (5) a theory on the part of the anthropologist about the way in which a group of people in fact behave; (6) a 'store-house of pooled learning'; (7) 'a set of standardized orientation to recurrent problems'; (8) 'learned behavior';

(9) a mechanism for the normative regulation of behavior; (10) 'a set of techniques for adjusting both to the external environment and to other men'; (11) 'a precipitate of history'.

(Geertz 1973: 4–5)

As for himself, Geertz states that he takes the notion of culture as

essentially a semiotic one. Believing, with Max Weber, that man is an animal suspended in webs of significance he himself has spun, I take culture to be those webs, and the analysis of it to be therefore not an experimental science in search of law but an interpretive one in search of meaning.

(*ibid.*: 5)

Thus the distancing characteristic of Geertz's methodological stance has an epistemological flair: the target of his polemic is a model of knowledge centred on an inventory of regularities and a recognition of rules.

Here one needs to observe that, during the course of the twentieth century, relationships between history and anthropology have also been affected by changing paradigms within both disciplines. In the 1960s, the structuralist anthropology of Claude Lévi-Strauss (1908–2009) expressly opposed a traditional form of history writing, engaged in reconstructing the intentional and voluntary agency of human beings, which he considered a superficial phenomenon; to that he opposed deep and unconscious social structures, which were impermeable to change. Over the same period, this model clearly influenced economic and social historians (in France and elsewhere), all occupied in collecting quantitative data and registering continuity, up to the point of speaking of a quasi-immobile history.

In subsequent developments, the scenario has significantly changed in both disciplines, to the extent that Roger Chartier (1996) has represented the whole itinerary of cultural history, as it has been practised at the École des Hautes Études en Sciences Sociales, as an ever-increasing breakaway from the certainties of serial history.[6] Therefore, in order to discuss the relationships between history and anthropology, we have to clarify what kind of history and what kind of anthropology we have in mind. The general remarks we have made so far would suggest, at least for a significant sample of authors, an inclination to common or parallel lines, influenced to a variable extent by the linguistic turn that has affected twentieth-century social sciences (discussed in the following chapters from several perspectives).

The bestknown example of Geertz's influence on historians is offered by his Princeton colleague Robert Darnton, a specialist of the history of the book in eighteenth-century France. His well-known essay (Darnton 1984), inspired by Geertz's own on the Balinese cock fight, narrated a cat massacre perpetrated by a group of Parisian artisans, which was meant partly as revenge, partly as a joke; it referred to folkloric material and literary sources, including some establishing a series of symbolic associations for the cat (in particularly with witchcraft and women's sexuality). The purpose – for an event as remote as this from our own sensitivity (involving as it did cruelty towards animals and laughter about it) – was to recover the meaning one can imagine the macabre ritual may have had for its perpetrators.

Both the anthropological model adopted by Darnton and its historical application to his case have raised some objections. Darnton's narrative is based on a contemporary diary, and some critics found that he did not treat his source problematically: literary conventions affect the writing of any text, making it fit into a given genre and address a specific audience; all this should be taken into account in their scholarly use and, as a result, the narratives told by sources should not be taken too literally. Levi thinks, in general, that the model of interpretive anthropology assigns an excessive role and freedom to the interpreter (the historian). By so doing, it ends up relying too much, for its efficacy, on the rhetoric and literary qualities of history writing (Levi 1985).

These remarks would be incomplete, however, if we did not register that similarities in procedure connect many of the aforementioned authors with one another, including the leading microhistorians: as is the case with Darnton's cats, a type such as the cripple (or, more generally, the theme of physical asymmetry) – registered in its occurrence in folklore, together with parallel motifs also found in the repertoire of fables – plays a role both in Davis's (1983) narrative of the story of Martin Guerre (the above-mentioned exchange of persons) and in the 'thick description' of the Sabbath included in Ginzburg's studies of witchcraft, from *The Night Battles* to the more ambitious *Ecstasies* (Ginzburg 1983, 1991).

Some of the histories of cultural history treat the phase of historical anthropology as an important but already concluded step in the evolution of the field (Burke 2008b);[7] a survey of the relationships between the two disciplines dates the decline in early modern historians' interest in anthropology to the 1980s (Gentilcore 2005). This was in no way a radical change of direction, however, and one reason why there is less insistence on the association between the two subject areas is simply because now a large part of it can be regarded as achieved and taken for granted. Suggestions deriving from anthropological research have come to inform the way we write the history of ritual (including the rituals of power), of gender relations, or of the exchange of gifts (in its symbolic, as well as economic, value); all this has left a permanent and easily recognizable impression.

As a conclusion to discussion on this point, it is worth adding that the challenges that a frank dialogue with anthropology may produce have not come to an end, and potentially might oblige historians to reconsider the very foundations of the notion of history as it is rooted in Western culture: ethnographical research has emphasized how different civilizations may not even share the idea of the past as a separate and concluded time dimension, but rather perceive past, present and future as implying one another (see Chapter 4 for the impact of writing on memory and the perception of time).[8] Memory itself has been a specific topic of cultural analysis, with seminal work on individual and collective processes of remembering conducted, in the 1920s and 1930s, by the psychologist Frederic Barlett and the sociologist Maurice Halbwachs (Green 2008).

Psychology is one of the other social sciences that have crossed the path of history in a variety of modes (here, too, to some extent depending on the changing paradigms within each discipline). The following chapters offer some samples, from Wundt's psychology of peoples (a source of inspiration, in the late nineteenth century, for **Karl Lamprecht**), to Blondel's collective psychology (which, some decades later, influenced Febvre) and Freudian psychoanalysis (a point of reference for Elias). In this case, too, the departure was uneasy, as history was naturally suspicious of psychology's attempt to reduce psychic life to a merely biological phenomenon, as well as of its tendency to propose itself as the ultimate explanation of human behaviour in general. In turn, with its devotion to the experimental method, psychology tended to regard historical documentation – not directly accessible to scientific investigation – at best as a secondary object of study. It has been said that time has allowed the overcoming of most of this antagonism (Gergen 1998). According to others, however, so far we can register mainly the misfortunes of psychohistory, even if further interaction between disciplines could produce mutual benefits: historians may helpfully refocus on the self; and cognitive neuroscientists may learn that the individual brain is not isolated and asocial (**Hunt** 2002). The German American historian **Peter Gay** (1985), who underwent additional personal training as a psychoanalyst, has offered one example of this kind, although this seems to remain rather exceptional.[9] A psychological dimension is present, for instance, in **Lyndal Roper**'s research on the European witch craze.

Summary

What is meant today by 'cultural history' is no longer the history of culture, in the ordinary sense of the term. As a field of enquiry, it is not defined by the breadth and limits of its object. It is not characterized by a unity of method either, if we consider that it is practised in a variety of different ways. The culturalist approach aims at cutting across the traditional subdivisions of the discipline of history (political, economic, military, and so on). Its nature and scope are comparable with those of social history, against which it is constantly measured. What distinguishes it from social history as it has ordinarily been practised is its focus on the other side of the coin: history from the viewpoint of the motives and meanings that individual and collective historical agents from the past gave to whatever they were doing, and to the contexts in which they operated.

This approach has emerged in its distinctiveness over the second half of the twentieth century. Its success is due partly to the effective employment, in interpreting past civilizations, of concepts and methods originating in other social sciences, and in particular in anthropological discourse.

Notes

1 As for the course on *Griechische Kulturgeschichte* he taught in 1872, which was published posthumously, it has been given alternatively as '*History of Greek Culture*' or '*The Greeks and Greek Civilization*' (Burckhardt 2002 and 1998).

2 Current German historiography tends to distinguish the recent trends from the older tradition by referring to the former as *neue Kulturgeschichte*.

3 Pier Paolo Viazzo (2000), an Italian scholar whose background and research career have given him familiarity with both disciplines, sketches a similar historical development of the relationships between history and anthropology. In sum, this is characterized by a phase of mutual indifference (roughly, the inter-war period), followed by one of rapprochement (starting from the 1950s and 1960s).

4 Filippo de Vivo (2010) has emphasized the difference existing between the total history of a village, which Le Roy Ladurie aimed at, and the paradigm adopted by the Italian microhistorians.

5 This is, for instance, the situation I can witness in Italy, where historians have made scarce use of it.

6 On the same process, see also Burke (1990: 79–85).

7 Also, Christiansen (2000).

8 Koselleck (1985: 3–20) has shown how the modern understanding of the Western tri-partition is the product of an early modern evolution in European 'temporalization of history', which saw the fading of prophetic expectations about the future of the world and its end, and their replacement by rational

forecasting. On the peculiarities of Western historical thinking in a global perspective, see also Rüsen (2002), with intercultural comments on ten theses put forward by Peter Burke.

9 There has also been the suggestion that what one could hope for is 'a three-way conversation between analysts, historians and anthropologists' (Burke 2007: 13).

2 Traditions and reinventions

Many introductions to cultural history devote at least a section – if not the entirety – of the text to a history of historiography. Thus the main methodological issues emerge from a survey of the forms actually taken, throughout time, by the practice of history writing that has most been inspired by a culturalist agenda. Via authors and texts from the historical literature of the past, the reader experiences the variety intrinsically characteristic of the genre, the debates that have accompanied its practice and the options still available for future research. In such narratives, writers have traced the origins of the discipline back to more or less distant precedents. Some went back to nineteenth-century Germanic *Kulturgeschichte*; some even further, to rediscover, for instance, the role played in the early eighteenth century by Giambattista Vico's philosophy of history. German historian Ute Daniel (2001: 195) has critically questioned the legitimacy of the whole operation of writing a history of cultural history. She warned against the tendency to justify one's method by assuming it has prestigious ancestors (*authority*), dates back to a remote time (*tradition*) and has remained virtually unchanged in its features (*identity*). Daniel has a point. It is difficult to claim that cultural history, as it is practised today, goes back more than a couple of decades. Nevertheless, this does not mean that retracing some characteristics of the way history has been conceived and practised by writers and schools from a less recent past is not worthwhile: a series of methodological choices they made have had consequences in the intervening time; others deserve re-examining in order to clarify issues of method in discussion today. Some references to episodes in the history of historiography will not be out of place, on the whole, both because current historical practice and methodological debates often recall more or less explicitly recent or remote precedents, and because the later forms of cultural history have been added to (rather than replaced) those of the previous tradition, which remains still alive in some practitioners.

As we have seen in Chapter 1, the protagonists of the French school of historical anthropology have explicitly indicated the eighteenth-century tradition of the history of mores as a specific precedent of theirs. As we have just suggested, Vico (1668–1744) represents an important figure in any attempt to retell the story of the forerunners of later studies in cultural history, if for no other reason, because the philosophy of history of this Neapolitan thinker – which inspired nineteenth-century developments of historicism – contemplates an evolution of human rationality along a series of stages (retracing the ages of man and the development of the individual's faculties), and assigns to language and its varying expressions a crucial role (Hughes-Warrington 2008: 375–80).[1]

After this preamble (soon after, if one considers that Vico died in 1744, and in the same year the third edition of his *New Science* was published), Voltaire's *The Century of Louis XIV* (1751) opened the second half of the eighteenth century. Rather than a traditional biography of the king, Voltaire offered the re-creation of the spirit of a glorious past epoch: the history of a nation, of its literary and artistic civilization, of its value system, populated by a series of characterizing key figures that left their impression on it. A few years later, the same French intellectual widened the perspective and, in order to propose in a volume the course of history preceding the period he had already treated, turned the gaze towards world history. He concentrated on the era beginning with the Middle Ages, and revealed significant curiosity and consideration for the civilizations of the Near and Far East, if compared with the standard universal histories, which were limited by the horizon of Greek-Roman and Judeo-Christian traditions. In its final version, his work would bear the title *Essay on the Manner and Spirit of Nations* (1753–69) and represent a mature finishing post of Enlightenment history writing for its choice of topics, vivid style and open challenge to previous modes of historiography. In truth, it would not be impossible to move quite a few steps backwards, only to realize that the putative father of the whole European tradition of historiography, the Greek Herodotus (fifth century BCE), when he surveyed the various people of the Mediterranean and Near East, described their customs with care (Hughes-Warrington 2008: 169–78). From this point of view, the odd-one-out is nineteenth- and early twentieth-century academic history writing inspired by positivism: centred on a narrower notion of historical fact – with emphasis on war and diplomacy, the powerful, and short-term developments – it significantly abandoned large territories as research fields for other social sciences, which in the same period were engaged in defining their status as disciplines. Thus, in a way, it was Rankean history that marked a break, which with hindsight can be read as a simple parenthesis.[2]

The nineteenth-century paradigm

The Swiss historian Jacob Burckhardt was the champion of a model of history of civilization that, in its narrative reconstruction of different epochs and contexts from the past, cannot renounce keeping together art and society, politics and culture. Since the time of its publication, his portrait of the Italian Renaissance, in particular, has remained the yardstick against which any subsequent interpretation of that period is measured – even (or particularly) when it tries to provide an overview, with interpretive keys for identifying turning points between adjacent periods, which inevitably have become the target of critiques and revision. This was the case for the alleged Renaissance 'development of the individual', on the background of an assumed medieval predominance of collective identities and lifestyles.

In a lecture delivered in Oxford in 1967, the art historian Ernst Gombrich made the critical claim that Burckhardt ultimately depended on G. W. F. Hegel's philosophy of history. Previous art critics, from Vasari to Winckelmann, had related the flourishing of art to the historical context that had favoured it; however, they had registered a subsequent change in such conditions and decadence in art. In Gombrich's opinion, it is with Hegel that decline is wiped out of the narrative: instead, we have a Spirit that is logically progressing, and manifesting itself in varying expressive forms.[3] Consequently, the characteristic feature of Burckhardt's historiography, and of his contemporaries and immediate successors, would be the search for the 'spirit of an epoch' (*Zeitgeist*) or 'spirit of a nation' (*Volksgeist*), which gives sense to individual works of art and other cultural manifestations.

Others found Gombrich's criticism unfair, and objected in particular to his suggestion of a specific Hegelian root for Burckhardt's notion of history. The Swiss historian not only, in general, distanced himself from philosophers; he also took repeated opportunities specifically to criticize the Hegelian perspective. He did so, for instance, in his correspondence, and in the introduction to his *Reflections on History*, where he wrote:

> We shall, further, make no attempt at system, nor lay any claim to 'historical principles'. On the contrary, we shall confine ourselves to observation, taking transverse sections of history in as many

directions as possible. Above all, we have nothing to do with the philosophy of history.

(Burckhardt 1943: 15; see Hinde 2000: 161)

By this he specifically meant that it is misleading to presuppose the 'anticipation of a universal plan', in which our era is considered as the fulfilment of all that preceded it, and the past as if it had just existed in preparation for what followed. The contrast is even more evident if we take into account that Burckhardt, rather than celebrating – like other contemporary intellectuals – the progress and achievements of the times he lived in, looked back with aristocratic nostalgia at a past, from which he felt the civilization of modern democracy represented a phase of decadence (Hinde 2000; Sigurdson 2004).

Following Burckhardt's work, the Germanic cultural area of the late nineteenth century became the theatre of debates, opposing the followers of political history against those of *Kulturgeschichte*. The precise terms and the varying tones and shades of those discussions are pre-dominantly of antiquarian interest today, and go beyond the scope of the present chapter. However, some characteristics of the history of culture as it was practised and put forward as a model for method in the environment of the German fin de siècle may prove interesting to consider, because these seem to anticipate, to some extent at least, features that would emerge again in the historiographical culture that developed between the two World Wars. Some of the issues do look dated today – for instance, the comparative autonomy each party recognized of cultural facts in relation to general history. On the other hand, it may be worth mentioning that the target of criticism by the followers of *Kulturgeschichte* was a political history intended as a reconstruction, if not celebration, of the historical triumph of the State (including a eulogy of the Prussian one). That the protagonists of cultural history defined their subject broadly, associating the study of culture with that of other factors, with particular attention to socio-economic conditions, also deserves mention. The economy and society were in fact ignored by official historiography, and combining them with the study of culture significantly anticipated a scenario from mid-twentieth-century France: the emergence of the history of mentalities from a predominantly socio-economic field of research (see Chapter 3). As lecturers, this group of scholars also tended – mainly – to teach different, parallel disciplines, to which they added history (or the history of culture): thus Burckhardt taught the history of art; Eberhard Gothein (1853–1923) mainly political economy. On the whole, their orientation remained marginal within the body of the German academic historians – a fact that bore consequences for their careers: Karl Lamprecht was the target of heavy criticism and practically ostracism from the profession; while Burckhardt was the protagonist of a twentieth-century rediscovery, rather than having considerable influence in his own time.

Expressly inspired by Burckhardt, Gothein significantly inherited and partly developed some of his favourite fields of enquiry by studying, among other topics, the Renaissance in southern Italy. Lamprecht, an advocate of cultural history as an alternative to the dominant political history, moved the emphasis towards a psychological meaning of the characteristic mentality of each epoch. Lamprecht's lectures were attended, among others, by **Aby Warburg**, who persevered in a cultural-historical vein that, with the intellectual exodus from Nazi Germany, was exported to the Anglo-Saxon world. More precisely, he was the reference point for the richest tradition in the study of iconography and iconology (Burke 2001a). In pioneering enquiries – from his graduation thesis on Botticelli's mythological paintings, whose classical and Renaissance literary sources he identified, to the analysis of the cycle of frescos in the Schifanoia Palace in Ferrara, which he interpreted in terms of con-temporary astrological doctrines – Warburg inaugurated a type of research engaged in reconstructing myths, figures and symbols, which materially embody a survival of fragments and motives of classical civilization, up to their reappearance in different forms in the modern world.

Beside Burckhardt, the other foreground figure in the practice of the history of culture at the turn of the twentieth century is the Dutchman **Johan Huizinga** – who also attended Lamprecht's lectures. In his view, 'the chief task of cultural history is the morphological understanding and description of the actual, specific course of civilizations' (Huizinga 1970: 51), avoiding excessive reliance on both the notion of development and a too schematic historical periodization.

The opinion Gombrich expressed in the aforementioned Oxford lecture was that we were still *in search* of cultural history. In his judgment, this was the case precisely because the Hegelian legacy – that is, the idea of the collective Spirit, with all its implications – was still influential, and we needed to get rid of it altogether. Consequently, Gombrich advocated a full appreciation of the role played by individuals. After registering similar developments in natural sciences, he observed: 'I hope and believe cultural history will make progress if it also fixes its attention firmly on the individual human being' (Gombrich 1969: 37). With this he implicitly adhered to the definition for humanities (or, as they were label-led at the time, 'moral sciences' – in German, *Geisteswissenschaften*) already put forward within late-nineteenth-century epistemological debates: the idea that rather than trying to imitate natural sciences, with their typical quest for regularities and laws, they had for their very nature a different object and method, assigning a distinctive importance to individual facts, unique *per se*, and their recognition and understanding. For his resistance to generalization beyond individuals, in today's terms we would not consider Gombrich a cultural historian.

Between idealism and materialism

A direct witness of the methodological debates German historiography went through in the late nineteenth century, Italian philosopher Benedetto Croce (1866–1952)[4] did not favour the idea of a history of culture as a somehow autonomous discipline. The hypothesis contrasted with his methodological choice for a total history. Still, in his idealistic notion of reality and of history, cultural aspects were destined to play an important role; and the actual application of Croce's method to the practice of history writing – both directly by himself and by the way he influenced the whole Italian historiographical culture of the first half of the twentieth century – would contribute to mark a tradition of historical studies as predominantly engaged on the front of intellectual history, conceived as the key that allowed privileged access to the identity of given historical phenomena and epochs.

One can take less for granted what role the Marxist tradition gave to cultural facts (for a synthesis, see Perry 2002). Although it, too, started off from Hegel's philosophy of history, Karl Marx's thought had subsequently turned it upside down in the direction of materialism. According to a position that the young Marx developed in his criticism of Hegel's philosophy, 'it is not the consciousness of men that determines their existence, but their social existence that determines their consciousness' (Marx 1971: 21). Writing history, therefore, was both, inextricably, a militant intellectual praxis that criticized the present state of things, and a study, in essence, of the socio-economic conditions of existence of human beings. In some of Marx's clearest statements, such an orientation excluded per se the mere possibility of a history of culture as an independent discipline. As Marx and Engels repeated in the *Communist Manifesto* (1848), the ideas of the ruling class are, in every epoch, the ruling ideas. An earlier formulation of this principle, expressed in their *The German Ideology* (composed in 1845–46, although published only posthumously), gave the following examples:

> If now in considering the course of history we detach the ideas of the ruling class from the ruling class itself and attribute to them an

independent existence, if we confine ourselves to saying that these
or those ideas were dominant at a given time, without bothering
ourselves about the conditions of production and the producers of
these ideas, if we thus ignore the individuals and world conditions
which are the source of the ideas, we can say, for instance, that
during the time that the aristocracy was dominant, the concepts
honour, loyalty etc., were dominant, during the dominance of the
bourgeoisie the concepts freedom, equality, etc. The ruling class
itself on the whole imagines this to be so.

(Marx and Engels 1965: 61)

Consequently, a history of philosophy, of art, of religion – as Hegel
had conceived them – that reviewed forms and orientations of individuals
and groups without relating them to the social interests they expressed
and represented, was meaningless:

The phantoms formed in the human brain are also, necessarily,
sublimates of their material life-process, which is empirically verifi-
able and bound to material premises. Morality, religion, metaphysics,
all the rest of ideology and their corresponding forms of consciousness, thus no longer retain the semblance of independence.
They have no history, no development; but men, developing their
material production and their material intercourse, alter, along
with this their real existence, their thinking and the products
of their thinking. Life is not determined by consciousness, but
consciousness by life.

(ibid.: 37–38)

Furthermore, to believe the pretence of the autonomy of culture
amounted to a distortion, a more or less deliberate eulogy of the
existing social order, thus falling into the category of what Marx
labelled as *ideology*. In fact, it was typical of the political, legal, cultural institutions of an epoch or historical setting (the 'superstructure',
a scaffolding over the economic 'structure', the latter providing the real
foundation of social order) to present themselves *as if* they were
objective and autonomous, whereas they depended on the governing
socio-economic forces, and contributed to the ensuring and reproducing
of their commanding role. To unmask this alleged independence,
and demonstrate its non-existence, was therefore the peculiar task of
historico-political critique.

This is not the right place for a detailed recounting of the course
followed by the Marxian tradition, whose intellectual history

intertwines with the political one of nineteenth- and twentieth-century workers' and socialist movements. It will be sufficient for our purpose to mention that the interpretation of the founder's thought that most closely adheres to economic determinism – what is commonly labelled as 'vulgar Marxism' – circulated but was not undisputed; and that trade unionist and political experiences could themselves allow individuals to discover and appreciate, on the contrary, the role that the agents' consciousness could play as a historical factor, as well as the weight of a political initiative, not mechanically determined by socio-economic dynamics.

Antonio Gramsci, a protagonist in the first phase of the history of the communist movement in Italy, stands out among the voices opposing the trend towards the debasement of the sphere of consciousness. His intellectual output was mainly consigned to notebooks he filled in while in jail or in confinement, under the fascist regime. It includes an emphasis on the role played by the political and cultural hegemony a social class manages to establish: social hierarchies do not only, or mainly, rest on economic unbalances due to the use of force to protect privilege; they are also based on the consensus they manage to obtain from the subordinate social groups. Thus, in Gramsci's historical analyses of the Italian case, special attention was paid to the role of the Church, its influence on the cultural history of the nation and on the Peninsula's socio-political map. As a more general consequence, intellectuals were given a high profile, both as mediators who ensured consensus with the given social order and/or as its questioners and underminers, who laid the foundation for the civic community of the future.

Gramsci's thought has enjoyed an international *fortuna* (as much as, or rather more than, Croce's), and continues to be influential in the literature still inspired by Marxism, or at least concerned to emphasize the relation between culture and social hierarchy: the notion of *cultural hegemony* was revitalized in the work of such late Marxists as **E. P. Thompson** and Raymond Williams, who questioned the notion of superstructure and clarified that of ideology. Gramsci's influence, and a re-use of his critical categories to interpret the postcolonial world, can also be seen in the Delhi-based group of subaltern studies – since the 1980s, one of the most representative schools of cultural studies.[5]

Both in the perspective of an idealistic historicism and in the form of a neo-Marxism like that of Gramsci (as we have seen), intellectuals were given an important role. Any socio-cultural history has therefore been confronted, for some time, with the task of writing their history: when was the modern intellectual born? To what professional groups of the past was allocated a similar position, and what place did they occupy in their respective worlds? One can set the aforementioned study of the creative élite of Renaissance Italy by Peter Burke (1972; see Chapter 1) in this perspective, as well as his use of the term *clerisy* to name the whole of the intellectual professions and the comparatively homogeneous social role they played in early modern Europe (Burke 2000). One of the most interesting episodes in this story is the notion of Republic of letters, a political metaphor adopted for self-representation, during the same period, in the sphere of the European intellectuals *avant la lettre*, that is, before the emergence, on the turn of the twentieth century, of intellectuals in the form we know them today (Bots and Waquet 1997).

A series of cultural–political confrontations – first of all, the 'affaire Dreyfus' – is the theatre in which, in the late nineteenth century, this figure is reshaped. A whole area of French study of late modern history is devoted to research on the history of the social group that develops from there – a significant portion of cultural history as it is practised in France today.[6] As for individuals and groups, it is clear that describing the emergence and evolution of cultural institutions is as important (Poirrier 2004: 131–44). This is another field in which essential pages in the European story have been written in the medieval and early modern periods – from universities, to courts, to Renaissance academies.

Twentieth-century developments

If we pass over the swings in themes and methods that prevail from time to time in each decade, the most serious test historical disciplines on the whole had to face over the past generation was the challenge of postmodernism. The term defines, although not unambiguously or without variations in use:

- on one side, a step in the development of social structures – with the coming of the societies we have taken to commonly call post-industrial, in reference also to the marginal role manufacturing has been playing in them, or at least in their geographical centres;
- on the other side, a cultural movement within the humanities, one that has conquered significant positions inside today's academia (particularly in the United States), and which is characterized by giving the relevant disciplines a distinctive *linguistic turn*. Its most comprehensive implication for historical research is a radical emphasis on the subjective component in the production of historical discourse, on various accounts converted into a tale whose techniques of composition do not differ significantly from those adopted in literary fiction (Jenkins 1997).

Although the consequent battles over the reality status of history are obviously important, they fall outside the specific scope of the present book. However, at least two related reflections rightly belong to cultural history – in fact, they are strictly intertwined with the development this approach to history has taken, and have to some extent marked its identity. One is the acknowledgment that the work of the protagonist of the postmodern orientation, **Hayden White** – in particular, his *Metahistory* (White 1973) – has provided an extraordinary contribution to the field of cultural history, by incorporating historiography itself as an object of study with unprecedented thoroughness and finesse. We now have at our disposal a model of unusual efficacy for analysing the historians' (and philosophers of history's) discourses as cultural artefacts characterized by the choices (and the conditioning factors) of their authors.

Secondly, any attempt – particularly, from the epigones – to push the new awareness of the textual nature of sources and historiography to the limit of dissolving any difference between fiction and reality, and claim that there is no reference outside the text, is inevitably destined to failure. On the contrary, the kind of history that has been advocated for, and written more widely and convincingly, is inextricably social and cultural at the same time (see Chapter 1).

Over the following four decades, White remained at the centre of the aforementioned methodological debates, brought to the extreme limits of revisionist negationism to which his positions have been questionably associated, up to the provocative thesis of the Holocaust being by its nature a narrative construction. The topic of his main work was, more specifically, 'the historical imagination in nineteenth-century Europe', that is, the different modes followed by a series of authors in organizing their narration of events. At the same time, in a series of volumes, French philosopher Paul Ricoeur (1913–2005) also analysed the relation between historical narrative and fiction tales, going back to the methodological reflection proposed on the subject in ancient thought, and particularly in Aristotle's *Poetics*. In White's approach, rhetoric is a crucial competence and perspective. In his reading of historians and philosophers of history, he emphasizes how the course of events they narrate, and seem to find in the very facts they reconstruct, in truth is the result of an intentional or unintentional narrator's selection: from the choice of the relevant facts to their disposition in a plot with a given course, a structure is largely superimposed on events, it sets them in a limited series of available narrative schemes (romance, comedy, tragedy and satire), and preferably ties them to one or another form of argumentation (formist, organicist, mechanistic or contextualist – according

to the way they focus on and connect the phenomena under investigation), as well as to an ideological orientation (anarchist, conservative,
radical or liberal).

On this aspect of the writing of history, *Metahistory* has offered a
reflection distinctively programmatic and systematic. Nevertheless, it
was not an isolated effort in that direction. For instance, as was
recently pointed out, the popular introduction to the study of history
published in the early 1960s by E. H. Carr (2001) included repeated
emphasis on the subjective nature of the historian's selection of facts. It
is not uninteresting that such a marked awareness of the limits of a
positivist faith in the objective nature of the events, as represented in
history writing, could partly result from the fact that Carr, on the
whole, was an outsider, a British diplomat and journalist turned author
of a monumental history of the Soviet revolution.

The most recent methodological debates have raised doubts over the
very possibility of historiography as an intellectual enterprise, and the
reliability of its outcomes. Cultural history can offer in its own way
some response to such doubts, in the form of a historical enquiry on the
criteria of truth – a history of truth, as it has been named (Fernández-
Armesto 1997). In it, one discovers that our doubts are anything but
new and that, rather than an evolution, what we have witnessed is the
resorting, in various combinations, to a constant series of criteria (the
truth one 'feels'; that respectively attested by authority, consensus,
reason or senses); and the best 'guide for the perplexed' is continuing
to refer to this multiplicity of sources: combined together, they correct
one another and allow one to avoid fundamentalism on one side
(the conviction that you hold the only truth, which naturally combines
with the conviction that everyone else is mistaken); and, on the other,
complete and radical scepticism (one that questions the very sense and
value of any research).

The lesson taught by the linguistic turn had, among other effects,
that of urging the most methodologically aware historiography to a
renewed sensitivity towards the history of language (see Chapter 3) and
consciousness of the rhetorical aspects of sources. If sound source criticism
has always taught whoever approaches sources to decode them by
considering the genre they belong to and the conventions within which
they were written, it is difficult to imagine that before the mid-1980s,
the narrative structure of a series of appeals to royal pardon might
become the main object of a monographic book. This is precisely what
Natalie Zemon Davis (1987) did in the case of sixteenth-century
France, by highlighting the strategies according to which writers of
appeals manufactured a reconstruction of crimes at the origin of the

sentence they were begging to condone. Reading the archival material in this perspective allows the author to shed light, among other points, on the peculiarities that such strategies acquire among particular agents, such as women. One could add that this new awareness and attention to the stylistic aspects of our historical documents is related to a growing interest in the history of communication and the media, of writing and reading as cultural practices, topics to which we shall return (Chapter 4). It is also clearly connected to a 'revival of narrative', that is, to a return by historians themselves to an intelligent use of narrative techniques, after the indigestion of data and tables that characterized the central years of the twentieth century (Burke 2001b; Roberts 2001).

In its own way, this turn reflects the hegemonic tendency of cultural history to put itself forward as the new form of a total history.

Summary

The roots of modern cultural history go back at least to Vico. Between the late nineteenth and early twentieth centuries, especially in the Germanic area, a new theoretical awareness concerning the study of culture came of age. It was accompanied by a historiographical gaze upon the worlds of the past that emphasized cultural factors such as lifestyle and modes of thought.

The linguistic turn during the second half of the twentieth century has been the most influential factor in this field, with varying outcomes in different cultural contexts and traditions of study; the textual nature of both sources and history writing has a newly acquired central role.

Notes

1 I do not suggest here that Vico had a major influence on eighteenth-century historical thought and practice; on the contrary, it is well known that his philosophy was the object of a later rediscovery.
2 We will return briefly to Leopold von Ranke and historical evidence in Chapter 4; see also White (1973: 163–90).
3 For an outline of his philosophy of history, see Hegel (1975).
4 For a portrait, see Hughes-Warrington (2008: 45–53); for a discussion of his philosophy of history see White (1973: 375–425).
5 Within a critical review of the historiographical category of 'mentality' (see Chapter 3), Burke (1997: 175) mentions it among the available alternative concepts.
6 As practised, for instance, by Jean-François Sirinelli, and engaging dedicated networks of scholars such as the Groupe de recherche sur l'histoire des intellectuels (see Poirrier 2004: 145–58).

3 Interwoven paths

As we have seen (Chapter 2), among the roots of today's cultural history, one could certainly recognize nineteenth-century, predominantly German-speaking *Geistesgeschichte* ('history of mind'). This also means that what lies behind it is a tradition of philosophical, literary and artistic historiography, which has been interested for centuries not only in portraying the profile and contribution of individual characters, but in identifying collective paths as well, followed by schools and movements. Thus that tradition inaugurated the retelling of an anonymous story of given, almost personified, linguistic expressions and forms of thought (such as concepts and ideas), and allowed and accustomed us to conceive them as having a life of their own. The degree to which these expressions and forms can be actually imagined independently from the authors and texts who adopt and appropriate them depends on the point of view, on the critical choices made by the observer; the same applies to the extent to which the whole sphere of mental and discursive experience can be regarded as determined by other factors of human existence, such as material, socio-economic factors. We have already mentioned (Chapter 2) that the Marxist interpretation expressly and unequivocally rules out any autonomy of cultural facts; in a more nuanced and complex way, many other scholars of different critical orientation have also postulated relationships between culture and society. Whatever the case, in the course of the twentieth century a number of different research directions have been established in this field. While relatively distinguishable, they have also repeatedly intertwined with one another.

The study of the relation between words and concepts, and of their variation through time, has been the object of more than one disciplinary approach. To sum up, one can focus on either pole of the relation and keep it still, while following the dynamics of the other. Thus in the history of ideas – a discipline with a historico-philosophical tradition – attention is concentrated on the side of the *signified* (to adopt, loosely, the dichotomy of Ferdinand de Saussure's theory of linguistics). Historical semantics, usually practised within the context of linguistic and literary studies, is, instead, anchored to individual terms (Saussure's *signifier*). The Austrian literary critic and linguist Leo Spitzer (1887–1960) provided a classic example of this approach with his semantic history of the idea of world harmony – a work originally published in the 1940s (Spitzer 1963). By comparison with these two approaches, a third perspective has been positioning itself somehow between, with the aim at considering words and problems together: the 'history of concepts' (in German, *Begriffsgeschichte*). In what follows, we will aim at clarifying the features of some of these research itineraries, and follow a selection of significant developments.

Intellectual history, history of ideas

As the label for an orientation, 'history of ideas' is unanimously considered as a creation of the American historian Arthur O. Lovejoy (1873–1962). During the 1930s, he offered a model of the method he had worked out in his study of the 'great chain of being', that is, the idea that the world forms an organic whole, disposed in a hierarchical order of perfection (Lovejoy 1970). In 1940, he founded the *Journal of the History of Ideas*, a platform that has since hosted a wealth of studies inspired by his view. The main characteristics of Lovejoy's method are, on one side, the reduction of ideas to minimal and independent units; on the other, the emphasis on research in them as an interdisciplinary enterprise.

The American historian did not offer an unambiguous definition of what should be taken as an *idea*. He left its types, even heterogeneous, to emerge from practice: they could range from principles to unconscious mental habits. He suggested, nevertheless, the chemical metaphor, by which complex concepts and principles had to be broken up into their basic components, which could be studied in their historical trajectories. A strength of this approach was the fact that it allowed the itinerary of ideas to be followed across disciplinary boundaries (from philosophy or religion to art or literature, and so on). Thus it helped to account for developments that would have been hard to understand within the limits of a single, specific field.

Lovejoy's model has not satisfied many critics, however, who were unconvinced by the existence of intellectual atoms, as such not subject to variation. He was also accused of privileging continuity over change, and not giving linguistic aspects an adequate role (the latter are, conversely, at the centre of the semantic approach). Nevertheless, Lovejoy himself proved to be more flexible as a practising historian than he was as a theorist. A variety of scholars refer more or less explicitly to a less rigidly conceived history of ideas; the orientation of the more recent intellectual history is also connected to it.

'Intellectual history' is a phrase that circulated in the United States at the beginning of the twentieth century. The intention, to sum up, was to superimpose a common marker on the separate itineraries of the histories of philosophy, science, art and literature. In parallel with the aims of the aforementioned history of ideas, the programmatic task here, too, was an overcoming of barriers and a retelling of the history of thought as a whole. After World War II, the expression had a revival and a limited additional diffusion in Europe; here, however, its use has remained marginal, both because the disciplines it hoped to blend together retained their independent life (in Italy, for instance, the history of philosophy), and because in other cultures alternative, largely equivalent phrases prevailed (in France, in the tradition of the *Annales*, 'history of mentalities' or 'historical psychology').

A field of enquiries that has demonstrated a distinctive dynamism and may exemplify intellectual history as it is practised today better than others is the history of political thought. One of its foremost representatives, the English historian **Quentin Skinner**, was inspired by the speech act theory formulated by the British philosopher John Langshaw Austin (1975). According to the latter's classification, in every utterance we should distinguish between what is said (locutionary act), what one aims at producing by saying it (illocutionary act – for instance, asking a question) and the resulting effect (perlocutionary act – in the given example, obtaining an answer). Consequently, intentions appear as a different and wider dimension from the mere identification of conceptual meanings: this dimension comes to directly refer to a performative sphere, what with words we mean (and/or manage) to do. In this perspective, in his analysis of a series of texts in the history of Western political thought, Skinner has tended to enquire about the authors' intentions: the researcher's task is not, therefore, limited to retracing the meaning of a text; s/he has expressly to ask why they chose to write and/or publish it.

Such questioning necessarily implies attention to the context – an emphasis that differentiates this approach from a more traditional philosophical historiography. On the whole, the latter considered ideas as if they had a life of their own, and left in the background, as less significant data, biographical information on the authors or other contextual elements. In examining their sources, Skinner and other representatives of this research orientation resort to a variety of techniques for the analysis of texts. They have particularly valued rhetorical aspects, first of all the assigning the work they examine to a given literary genre, which influences a series of stylistic features and also affects the forms of its reception by the reading public. In this mode, for instance, Maurizio Viroli (1998) has proposed an innovative interpretation of a classic that has been studied many times over – Machiavelli's *The Prince*.

While the panorama of intellectual history in the Anglo-Saxon world is characterized by studies (predominantly by scholars working individually) of the vocabulary of specific authors, considered as a whole, in the German-speaking area the domain has been occupied largely by collective and systematic works, in which particular, relatively isolated concepts have been brought into focus. In this field, since the 1970s, the study of historical semantics has regained substance, and the history of concepts has acquired its definition.

Two multi-volume reference works – both launched in the 1970s and by now completed – have proved the most representative products of this approach: a historical dictionary of philosophy, edited under the direction of Joachim Ritter and Karlfried Gründer (1971–2005); and a historical lexicon of German socio-political language, edited by Otto Brunner, Werner Conze and **Reinhart Koselleck** (1972–97). For the latter work, the period from the eighteenth to the twentieth century was expressly chosen because that epoch saw the emergence of modern meanings of the political and social vocabulary, to the extent that its earlier semantic history was forgotten; language was therefore examined in its interaction with the social and political transformations that have shaped the modern world.

When do concepts vary? How often, how quickly, how radically? In what relationship is their variation with continuity or change in the reality they refer to? There are almost infinite possibilities, and no generalization would be appropriate. Koselleck (1994) suggested an elementary but useful model featuring four main scenarios:

- unchanged concepts and realities;
- concepts and realities changing in comparative synchronicity and mutual correspondence;
- changing concepts, while the realities they refer to remain constant;
- concepts that remain constant, despite the change in the realities they refer to.

For each situation, significant examples could be offered; if we bear the scheme in mind, we can orientate ourselves and be aware of the scenario we are facing on any given occasion. To exemplify a situation that changes while concepts remain the same, Koselleck recalls the case of Marxism, a doctrine that had to deal (and not without difficulties) with political and economic developments its founder could not foresee; naturally, something similar could be said of many other periods and circumstances. Marc Bloch had already expressed a fairly similar view:

> changes in things do not by any means always entail similar changes in their names. Such is the natural consequence of the tra-ditionalist character of all language, and of the lack of inventiveness common to most men
>
> (Bloch 1992: 131)

thus recalling the historical dimension of language (to which we will return below, in this chapter).

The forms of diffusion of particular ideas and mental attitudes are among the aspects that are subject to potentially different interpretations. In his contribution to an international conference of historical studies held in the mid-1990s, Robert Darnton traced the diverging of two schools of intellectual history, which he dated to the 1970s: on one side was the analysis of discourses as practised by the 'Cambridge school' (Skinner and other historians of political thought of similar orientation, such as John Pocock); on the other was diffusion studies, which in France had concentrated on the history of the book (see Chapter 4). With reference to the latter group, Darnton talked ironically of a model of explanation that

> operated like a French filter coffee machine: it assumed that ideas trickled down from an intellectual elite to the general public and that once they became absorbed in the body politic they stimulated a revolutionary spirit.
>
> (Darnton 1995: 179)

This image may effectively suggest how limiting excessive simplification (of the processes of circulation of ideas) may prove – and how com-plex, on the contrary, is the reality that historiographical models should describe; it may also remind us that it is fitting to be aware of the existence of such models, and of their often implicit adoption. The fact remains that Darnton's coffee machine is a caricature, and the scho-lars who are meant to be represented by it would not recognize them-selves in the portrait: from reception theorists and literary theorists, historians have learnt to pay attention to the modes of appropriation and adaptation that make the circulation of texts and ideas anything but a one-way communication, accepted by passive receivers (see Chapter 4).

History of mentalities

The phrase 'history of mentalities' came into use in France at the end of the 1950s (Poirrier 2004: 45–73). Nevertheless, it identified a type of approach that is usually ascribed to the two founding fathers of the French historical school: Marc Bloch and Lucien Febvre. Frequently associated, in the vocabulary typical of the *Annales*, with ideas ('history of ideas and mentalities'), the study of mentalities expresses the aspiration to bring back a common feeling, and that is also meant in opposition to the predominance of the elite. In this sense, it represents the intellectual side of the coin of the historiographical rediscovery and appreciation of the subaltern classes, pursued by social history. The term *mentalité* was current in France in the first quarter of the twentieth century in a variety of contexts, from common usage (Marcel Proust registered this) to the specific sphere of various branches of the humanities. In particular, the association between 'mentality' and 'primitive' appeared around that time as a title of books published both by ethnologists (Lévy-Bruhl 1923) and by psychologists (Blondel 1926, with a preface by Lévy-Bruhl). The aim is to explain the operating of cultural functions regarded as pre-logical and as dominated by emotional behaviour, unsurprisingly also associated with the minds of children (Revel 1986a). Implicit in the perspective of the history of mentalities is a marked distancing from the object observed: 'In other words, to assert the existence of a difference in mentalities between two groups is to make a much stronger statement than merely asserting a difference in attitudes' (Burke 1997: 162). From the perspective typical of intellectual history, the history of mentalities diverged, among other aspects, on account of its inclusion of forms of sensitivity as well as of rational categories.

There is a general consensus about the fact that Bloch's *The Royal Touch* (Bloch 1973) and Febvre's *The Problem of Unbelief in the Sixteenth Century* (Febvre 1982) represent two key accomplishments and reference points in this field. Bloch, a medievalist, asked how was it possible for the belief in the healing power of the touch of the kings of France and England to emerge and last for centuries. He presented the underlying magical notion of power as part of a society's symbolic stock. A sociological perspective is even more visible in Bloch's subsequent study of feudal society, where he tried to distinguish between the ideologies of different social groups and to present the epoch's typical mental structures against a background of influential demographic and environmental circumstances (Bloch 1989). Febvre, a scholar of the early modern period, took the literary work of Rabelais as a starting point, to ask whether atheism was a possibility in Renaissance culture, in both its characteristic conceptual structures and its forms of sensitivity. The background of his enquiry is more openly psychological.[1] This is not the appropriate place to discuss the reliability of Febvre's conclusions. It will be sufficient to mention that he regarded religious beliefs as unavoidable in sixteenth-century Europe – a position that seems disproved by the wealth of sources available and examined today, when the majority of specialist scholars of atheism and unbelief disagree with him. What matter here, rather, are the new terms in which he formulated the problem and devised a method appropriate to investigate it.

An outline of the methods and aims of this research orientation was drawn in the early 1960s by **Georges Duby**, a medievalist who, over the following thirty years, was among the foremost historians, also engaged in the direction of such collective enterprises as *A History of Women in the West* (Duby and Perrot 1992–94) and the *A History of Private Life* (Ariès and Duby 1987–91). Together with the early modernist Robert Mandrou (another prominent figure who took up Febvre's heritage and developed the history of mentalities both as a practising historian and with reflections on method), Duby had recently published *A History of French Civilization*, which was put forward as a model in the field (Duby and Mandrou 1965). The French historian opened with the statement that historiography had been, by choice, psychological from its very beginning, with its questioning of the motives and passions that influence human agency. He subsequently offered an explanation of mentality as a phenomenon rooted in psychology, and acknowledged the contribution history could obtain from social psychology. The time perspective Duby outlined was especially the *longue durée* – continuity and slow movements, a background to more short-lived processes and events, and a basis for their understanding.

It was a question, among other tasks, of making an inventory of myths, beliefs and symbols; without losing sight of the material conditions of human life that influence them, mental factors also deserved comparative autonomy and adequate attention (Duby 1961). At that time, scholars coming from social history, including several of Marxist orientation, converted to the field of mentalities without abandoning their interest in social hierarchy and the relationships between living conditions and world representations: they found that, compared with the old category of *ideology*, the new one was more versatile and effective in opening up unexplored territory to research (Vovelle 1990; see also Chapter 2).

Philippe Ariès was another key figure in this approach. He is particularly known as a scholar who for a long time explored human attitudes towards life and death.[2] In a historiographical and methodological assessment of the history of mentalities, he began from a historical anecdote he in turn borrowed from Febvre (Ariès 1988). The protagonist of the story is Francis I (King of France from 1515 to 1547). Early in the morning, he was leaving the company of his mistress to reach his castle incognito. As he was walking past a church, the bells rang and the sovereign, moved, stopped to attend Mass and pray with devotion. One could offer various explanations for the complexity of his behaviour: a sudden remorse? Insincere religiosity? In the end, it is our modern sensitivity that sees an incompatible contradiction in that sequence of gestures and behaviour; the perspective of the history of mentality has in its very agenda the will to avoid this type of anachronism, and accept the simultaneous possibility of such practices and feelings in human beings who lived in a time or space other than that of the observer. Febvre proposed, as a similar case, that of Francis I's own sister, Marguerite de Navarre, who was at the same time the author of spiritual poems and of salacious tales.

To clarify the concept of mentality, Ariès offers some more telling examples. The notion of time is one of particular relevance: such research as Jacques Le Goff's on the cultural sphere of medieval Western Europe has emphasized the changes that progressively saw the waning of the 'Church's time', and the simultaneous emergence of the 'merchant's time'. Demographic phenomena, which post-war historiography had investigated through the use of statistical tools, offered further subject matter for study. For instance, analysis of a combination of quantitative and qualitative sources allowed scholars – among them Ariès – to suggest, by inference from the dynamics of the birth rate, that at the end of the eighteenth century France witnessed a novel diffusion of contraceptive methods, which signalled an implicit change in religious and moral attitudes.

A few years before Ariès, Le Goff (1985 – originally published in 1974), another key player in French historiography, had proposed an assessment of the history of mentalities. He treated it as a research orientation still at a pioneering stage. Nevertheless, he labelled it as 'a history of ambiguities' and asked whether the phrase was endowed with sufficient conceptual consistency and a corresponding scientific reliability. His answers were not negative, however, and the French historian could appreciate as a strong point the very vagueness of this research perspective (of its boundaries as well as of its qualities), by claiming that it conferred a special and advantageous flexibility. Notwithstanding their positive tone, Le Goff's remarks questioned the methodological preconditions of this field of enquiry. Many others followed suit over subsequent years.

Among the limits which the history of mentalities, as a perspective, has long demonstrated are: its tendency to homogenize all the components of a given culture, by accentuating the weight of consensus over dissent and underestimating the most original cultural products of an epoch; its limited capacity of account for change, by insisting on the long-term and quasi-immobile mental structures; and a tendency to an evolutionistic ethnocentrism, which may present the mentalities of the past sympathetically, but in the end regards them as inferior (less true or less effective) than the observer's. The latter is undoubtedly an attitude from which the scholar should refrain. Nevertheless, it has more or less explicitly been adopted by recent historians who have blamed the mentality of men and women of the past as responsible for actually failing them in their hopes of improving living conditions.

In partial reply to these objections, it has been noticed that some French historians have shown sensitivity to the varying of cultural forms between different social groups, and have been able to recognize more than one mentality as simultaneously present not only in a given society, but even in the same individual, as we have just seen in the case of Francis I (Chartier 2001).[3]

Towards the end of the 1990s, Peter Burke (1997), from whom we have borrowed the above summary of the recognized limits, concluded his survey of the question by suggesting some proposals for a reformulation of the history of mentalities. They included a stronger emphasis on the element of interest, which may significantly help explain the survival or decline of a number of mentalities; an attention not limited to the 'atoms' of which thought is composed, but also directed to the varying historical structures that organize them (paradigms, schemata or systems); and an appreciation of the role played by language, and particularly metaphors and symbols, in shaping the way we think. This is the case for such metaphors as the body politic, studied by Ernst Kantorowicz (1997) and destined to influence the history of political doctrines in the long term (contrary to the sovereign's physical body, it was immortal); or, again, the omnipresence of the imagery of machines in seventeenth-century thought, or the juristic model that suggested the existence of 'laws' of nature.

Jack Goody is among the scholars who have expressed the most radical criticism of this orientation in history writing. On one side, he denounces the fact that all alleged revolutions in attitudes – such as that towards childhood postulated by Ariès, or that towards the natural world suggested by Keith Thomas (for both see Chapter 4) – are faulty on account of a lack of comparison: in order to be able to support their claims, the respective authors should document – much more substantially than has been done so far – the uniqueness of the attitudes in question if compared with those typical of previous historical periods, and/or of civilizations other than the one examined. On a more general level, Goody blames those explanations of historical phenomena that relate them to a particular mentality (as the 'Greek genius' supposed to be responsible for the success of the West, or any sort of *Zeitgeist*), because to face the singularity of a historical experience in such terms produces a vicious circle, which does not explain anything (Pallares-Burke 2002: 15–16, 24; see also Chapter 4).

A characteristic feature of the early stages of the history of mentalities was the use of the metaphor of the 'mental toolbox' (*outillage mental*), introduced by Lucien Febvre. The starting premise is the wish to avoid anachronism, by acknowledging the distance that separates us from the world experience of our ancestors, by learning lessons from both anthropology and psychology. The instruments or 'tools' in question, therefore, included 'the vocabulary and syntax, the categories of perception and sensitivity, mental habits, as well as knowledge and concepts' (Revel 1986b: 497).

Language is necessarily the first and most indispensable of such tools. It consists of 'the various means of expression individuals receive from the social groups in which they live, which frame all their mental life' – a research topic to be investigated starting from 'a systematic and chronological inventory of words' (Duby 1961: 953). The quantitative dimension posed a similar issue: what kind of familiarity did individuals belonging to different social and cultural groups of the past have with the world of numbers, and how interested were they in the measure of anything? In the 1930s, as editor-in-chief of the *Encyclopédie Française*, Febvre entitled its first volume precisely *L'Outillage mental*. It was meant as a general introduction to a work planning to classify the whole of human activities. He declared the task in the following terms, thus listing the areas the volume would cover:

firstly we will evoke and describe the three instruments of liberation and appropriation man has forged for himself: *logical thinking*, *language*, and the language of science, *mathematics*, this magnificent effort by reason to conceive the universe as a web of relations and functions.

(Febvre 1937: 1.04.12)

Febvre's language and tone reveal a trust in reason's potential and a pride in belonging to a civilization informed by it, in terms that inevitably appear distant from us today.

Symbols and representations

Since the 1990s, French historiography has spoken less in terms of mentalities, and has set itself the target of exploring such alternative entities as representations and the collective imagination. To a certain extent, what has changed is the name rather than the thing, and both historical research and publishing in the field proceeded along pathways rather similar to those followed previously. Nevertheless, the expressions in use have something to say about the methodological options and areas of enquiry that historians mostly favoured.

The study of the symbolic universe represents a ground where cultural history, literary and artistic criticism and psychology meet (Decharneux and Nefontaine 1998). The philosophy of symbolic forms, developed during the 1920s by the German thinker Ernst Cassirer (1874–1945) (Daniel 2001: 90–101; Boyd 1999: 183–84), which takes the creation of such structures of meaning that shape perception as distinctive of human beings, was the most systematic effort to represent this dimension of our existence. Among the subsequent generation, the German art historian **Erwin Panofsky** moved along this path, with studies that have considerably influenced the interpretation of symbolism in the visual arts. The category of the imaginary (French *imaginaire*) is above all connected to the theoretical reflection and cultural initiatives promoted by the French philosopher Gilbert Durand (1921–). It has been fairly popular with historians interested in the interpretation of myths and legends, taken as the expression of a collective unconscious, more or less directly inspired by Carl Gustav Jung (1875–1961) and his depth psychology: from the notion of archetype, to the postulate that the psychic experience of the individual is predisposed and influenced by that accumulated, from generation to generation, by humankind as a whole from the most remote of times (Wunenburger 2003). The field is immense, if one considers the elements that have been counted within it:

> the curiosity for horizons too distant in time and space, for unknowable lands, for the origins of humans and nations; the anxiety and anguish inspired by the unknown of the future and of the present; the awareness of the experienced body, the attention paid to the involuntary motions of the soul – to dreams, for instance; questioning about death; the periodicity of desire and its

repression; social constraint, generating a staging of forms of evasion or refusal, by listening to or reading of the utopian narrative, by images or play, festivals or the performing arts.

(Patlagean 1988: 307)

Lucian Boia – a protagonist of cultural history in Romania who is close to the approaches typical of French historiography – offers another significant example of a scholar who has both reflected on *imaginaire* as an interpretive tool (Boia 1998) and applied it to a broad variety of topics (those explored in his books available in English include longevity, and the weather: Boia 2004, 2005). The philosophical background of imagination was insightfully explored by Gaston Bachelard (1884–1962), who examined this human experience in general and its application to the fundamental elements: earth, water, air and fire ('Imagination allows us to leave the ordinary course of things. Perceiving and imagining are as antithetical as presence and absence. To imagine is to absent oneself, to launch out toward a new life', Bachelard 1988: 3).

The notion of representation (Chartier 1999a; Gil 2010) – itself an object of historical enquiry, considering that it has been used differently through time – has come to mark the whole level of reality distinctively observed by cultural history: rather than the world's structure and actual dynamics, its images. This does not mean that cultural phenomena are not real in their own way, and leaves open a complex and fundamental question: what relationship exists between the social and the cultural (a bogus problem only for the radically revisionist postmodernists, who do not believe that anything exists outside texts – see Chapter 2).

Different systems of representation predictably reproduce, articulate and interact with reality in different ways. This can be clearly experienced for different linguistic domains (see the closing section of the present chapter) as well as for separate disciplinary fields. A characteristic example of intersection between the symbolic sphere and social stratification is the study of the historical forms of representation of social hierarchy itself. A classic case of this is the idea of the tri-partition of premodern society into a religious, a military and a working order, for which the French comparative philologist Georges Dumézil (1898–1986) postulated Indo-European roots, and which Duby (1980) has studied for the medieval West.[4]

With a term borrowed from social theory, historians have talked of *subcultures* to define the internal subdivisions one can find within a given socio-cultural system: worlds within worlds, that is, groups characterized by comparatively independent worldviews and codes of conduct (Gentilcore 2002).

If we move our gaze from the vertical socio-cultural differences to the horizontal ones distinguishing cultures or civilizations from one another, representations of the Other provide the corresponding field of enquiry. The area has been subject to a variety of cultural influences – among them psychoanalysis – and has had a particular development in the study of the effects of geographical discoveries. In this sphere the complexity of cultural encounters, with consequent, different forms of acculturation and hybridity, has emerged more clearly than in the past. Many scholars have worked on related topics: among the most influential one should mention at least **Stephen Greenblatt**'s analysis of European responses to 'the wonder of the New World' (Greenblatt 1991) and **Michel de Certeau**'s reading of the French tradition of writing, from Montaigne to Lafitau (Certeau 1980, 1986: 67–79).[5]

An assessment is now possible of the variety of objects that are hybridized; of the variety of terms and theories invented to discuss cultural interaction (imitation and appropriation, accommodation and negotiation, or cultural translation, as well as creolization and syncretism); of the variety of situations in which encounters take place; of the variety of possible responses to unfamiliar items of culture; and of the variety of possible outcomes or consequences of hybridization over the long term (Burke 2009a). A whole tradition of historical phenomena and ways of analysing them stands behind the most recent developments and theoretical awareness.

A not unambiguous category, which for some time served to regroup the study not only of European expansion but also of Asian and African history independently from cultural encounters, was that of 'overseas history'. Although the very definition of the subject and the rationale of keeping different areas of research together under such a headline were questionable, it worked after 1945 as a fairly value-free conceptual framework for the study of world histories (Wesseling 2001). However, decolonization changed the context and sense of world history once and for all. Postcolonialism and subaltern studies have questioned the privileged role played by Europe and the West in shaping the very nature of the historical enterprise (Duara 2002; Gunn 2006: 156–81). Even the history of nations can increasingly and effectively be conceived and practised in multicultural terms (Gabaccia 2002). 'World history' is now specifically intended as the

> historical scholarship that explicitly compares experiences across the boundary lines of societies, or that examines interactions

between people of different societies, or that analyses large-scale historical patterns and processes that transcend individual societies. (Bentley 2002: 393)

The fact that a whole new dimension for history and cultural analysis has been opened up by concentrating on the nature and implications of human mobility, has led American critic Stephen Greenblatt (2010) and others to put forward the notion of *mobility studies,* a perspective that considers physical movement and its conditions as a necessary ground for the proper understanding of spatial metaphors, and includes interest in contact zones, in the sensation of rootedness, in the fact that some movements are virtually invisible, as well as in the tension between individual agency and structural constraint.[6] The latter point has proved particularly fruitful in inspiring a string of narratives of individuals whose lives spanned 'between worlds', their displacement potentially triggering religious conversion or other identity troubles (Davis 1995, 2006; **Colley** 2007; **Frijhoff** 2007).[7]

By evoking Greenblatt's name, one is also reminded that, naturally, literature (together with art) represents a privileged field for the distinctive representations of any given culture. The work of Greenblatt, and the journal *Representations* he co-founded, offer some of the clearest and bestknown examples of the difference between traditional literary historiography and an approach in terms of cultural history. They regard culture as a network of signs, and interdisciplinarity as the only fruitful way to interpret it; history and literature as mutually imbricated (neither are texts independent of their authors and readers, nor is the past completely detachable from the discourse that narrates it) (Greenblatt 2005).[8]

Languages, discourses

As we have seen earlier in this chapter, language itself is the most important tool history writing has aimed at exploring, as Bloch too once hinted. The following observations by his colleague Febvre went in the same direction:

> What in fact can we get from a study of vocabulary? Not very much as far as sentiments are concerned. Sometimes it makes it possible to isolate and grasp certain conditions in the fundamental existence of the men who created the vocabulary in question. To take an example that is more than classical, it can enable us to make clear the agricultural element in words in a language such as Latin,

where *rivalité* (rivalry) has taken its name from the argument between neighbours claiming the same irrigation channel, *rivus*; where the outstanding quality of a man, *egregius*, is compared with the excellence of the animal that is removed from the flock or herd, *e grege*, to be looked after separately; where the weak man, *imbecillus*, evokes the idea of a plant without support, *bacillus*; where the notion of joy, *laetitia*, remains tied up with the idea of fertilizer, *laetamen*.

(Burke 1973: 20)

The social history of language, originally set by linguists, has more recently been fully appropriated by historians as an important dimension of their research. In the case of early modern Europe (although the dynamics in many other chronological and geographic settings are comparable), competition between languages is a decisive horizon for many relevant phenomena: from the emerging of vernacular languages and the forms of survival of Latin, to the standardizing processes; from the tendency to mix different languages, to repeated reactions in the direction of purism (Burke 2004b).

As suggested at the beginning of this chapter, the history of science is one area of traditional history of culture which cultural history has taken to significantly rewrite (Daniel 2001: 361–79; Poirrier 2004: 233–43). The previously dominant approach to this field of study can be effectively exemplified with the work of Alexandre Koyré, the Russian-born philosopher who read the seventeenth-century scientific revolution in terms of geometrization of space and mathematization of the laws of nature – that is, purely in terms of intellectual history, thus practically ignoring the whole social and economic environment from which that story emerged. In contrast, today the emphasis is much more on the reconstruction of communities, of scientific practices and institutions (for an example, see Jardine *et al.* 1996; the work of **Lorraine Daston**, **Paula Findlen**, **Lisa Jardine** and **Ludmilla Jordanova** could also be cited). At the opposite end of the interpretative spectrum, research has gone as far as proposing a 'social history of truth' (such is the title of a book by American historian of science Steven Shapin, 1994). If the outcome of the latter approach has not convinced many critics so far, it is predictable that over the next few years other scholars will follow similar paths.[9]

In the meantime, research on the historical forms of knowledge has tried to avoid producing a history with hindsight of their periodical replacement, from the view point of the most recent acquisitions of science and technology. Thus the culture of the past can be rediscovered also in the formal structures that organized its content and influenced the range of options. British historian **Stuart Clark** (1997) has done so for early modern European witchcraft, by showing that the predominant conceptual universe – with its mutually implying binary oppositions – made sure that belief in its real existence was not simply possible, but even unavoidable. A similar relating of knowledge to its cultural context is also made more urgent by the awareness of the importance of scientific traditions other than the Western one – as demonstrated by Joseph Needham (1900–95) in his study of the Chinese.

Beside analysing the variety of these discursive practices, historical research (in parallel to what the histories of philosophy and of science do on one side; cultural anthropology on the other) is also interested in identifying relations between different systems, the turning point they experienced as well as the elements of continuity. In an important, though not widely known contribution, Erwin Panofsky (1962) referred to the Renaissance redefinition of the nature and boundaries of academic disciplines as a 'decompartmentalization'. In the process, a philosophical orientation such as neo-Platonism and such cultural practices as astrology, magic and alchemy played a key role by questioning the very foundations of traditional knowledge. It is from that reshuffling of the hierarchical order of disciplines that the new natural sciences emerged.

American philosopher of science Thomas Samuel Kuhn (1922–96; see Hughes-Warrington 2008: 210–19) is the author of a much more influential interpretation of the nature and development of the epistemological ruptures that produce scientific revolutions – a model he proposed both on a theoretical level and as applied to the specific, key case of Copernicus (Kuhn 1957, 1970). His fundamental thesis is that, in the history of science, one sees an alternation between periods of 'normal science', during which knowledge accumulates according to shared practice and within a framework on which the scientific community agrees, without seriously questioning the postulates of the entire system; and periods of crisis when, conversely, in order to accommodate new acquisitions, the whole reference structure of knowledge needs rebuilding. The pivotal concept adopted in this description is that of *paradigm* – one that rapidly came to be used also among historians (and consequently has been regularly appearing in the present volume).

Kuhn did not provide a fixed definition of the term, to the extent that some scholars have applied themselves to the exercise of counting in how many different senses he talked of paradigms. Generally, however, it is meant as the series of metaphysical presuppositions, theoretical orientations and experimental procedures that characterize the scientific community of a given epoch. As noted, normally new acquisitions can find room within the dominant system, or else require only limited adjustments. A scientific revolution is the result of a situation in which a paradigm shift is imposed by the amount of data the old framework is unable to account for, when substantial revision is required for an adequate explanation. The subject of intensive debate, Kuhn's model has been found to overestimate the degree of scientific consensus existing in any epoch (is there always such a thing as 'normal science'? For that matter, is there one at any time?), as if conflict between alternative paradigms occurred only in periods of crisis and transition. It also seems to take little consideration of the external factors that may influence the development of science.

On this front, the epistemology of Michel Foucault has had a unique influence: the 'history of the systems of thought', which the French intellectual adopted as a title for his courses at the Collège de France, expresses more clearly than any other statement the programme of this field of enquiry. It is also a highly original perspective, and the categories devised by Foucault have not often become standard currency among other historians.[10]

He frequently adopted a vocabulary that acquires a particular meaning in the context of his writing. This is the case for his whole research on knowledge, which he labelled as 'archaeology'; or again for the 'analysis of discourse' he conducted according to modes one could profitably compare to linguistics, but that have the distinctive feature of being fastened to a reflection on the range of possibilities of any statement in a given intellectual framework. Such is the nature of a key term of Foucault's, such as *episteme*.

An ancient Greek noun indicating scientific knowledge, in Foucault episteme defines the implicit system of rules within which, in any specific socio-cultural context, various 'discursive formations' are possible. He particularly employed the category in *The Order of Things* (Foucault 2002), a study of successive systems of thought – each defined by a group of typical disciplines and shared methodological orientation within a given epoch – which postulates significant turning points at both chronological ends of the early modern period. As a point of departure, the reader encounters the tendency, characteristic of Renaissance culture, to interpret the world in terms of similarities and correspondence. The seventeenth and eighteenth centuries witnessed the predominance of the category of representation; Linnaeus's botanical and zoological classifications offer an example of the way it operated. The human being as the actual object of enquiry emerges at a subsequent phase, with the birth of human sciences. Between these different stages one notices discontinuity, rather than transition; for his emphasis on rupture (French *coupure*, 'break, cut'), Foucault was inspired by the epistemology of Bachelard.

Foucault also displayed a similar interest in following the story of the formation of various disciplinary fields of knowledge, and of the conflicts between them, within the lectures he gave at the Collège de France – for instance, the case of medicine and law in the yearly course he devoted to the abnormal (Foucault 2003). His *History of Madness* (Foucault 2006) – also known in an abridged English version with the title of *Madness and Civilization* – besides the narrative of the 'Great Confinement' that led to the birth of the asylum, had already emphasized how knowledge and power labelled and treated as foolish a variety of types of individual and forms of behaviour, and how that variety altered through time (on this front, Georges Canguilhem's problematization of concepts of 'normal' and 'pathological' had been highly influential for him).

After their appearance on the market of ideas, Kuhn's paradigm and Foucault's episteme have been frequently compared and applied (jointly or separately) to a multiplicity of fields of theoretical and historical enquiry. They clearly overlap to a considerable extent: both authors and concepts illustrate how knowledge is based on some subjective and ultimately transitory premises, although Foucault – who also applies his observations to a wider range of disciplines – seems more aware that such premises may be unconscious. Also, both appear to have moved, during the course of their research, from an initial emphasis on the uniqueness of a dominant paradigm/episteme to the recognition of the potential and historically experienced coexistence of a plurality of them (here again, epistemic conflict and pluralism play a larger role in the context of Foucault's understanding and critical attitude).

Cultural history as a whole has sometimes been accused of being more able to account for continuity than change (we have already met this objection in the specific case of the history of mentalities). We can understand this critique better if we consider a tangible risk which cultural historians run: by distancing their object of enquiry as other, and borrowing methods from such social sciences as anthropology – for which the timescale has limited importance, and what matters most are the connections that synchronically link the various components of a system – past systems of thought may appear clearly in their consistency, whereas their gaps and variations may remain shadowed. This has also been observed about the critical tools devised by Kuhn and Foucault (despite the fact that, as we have seen, both expressly engaged in efforts to understand change). A few more critical suggestions in the direction of understanding change have been offered by the study of cultural diffusion: we will return to the subject at the end of Chapter 4 when reviewing the history of the book and of reading.

Summary

Though not identical to intellectual history, to the history of ideas or to that of concepts, cultural history shows clear connections with all these areas. It may be said that, during the 1970s and 1980s, the history of mentalities represented one of its main incarnations. That approach, however, is considered obsolete today.

One of cultural history's most distinguishing trends can be identified in the growing attention to the characteristic discourses of the different disciplines and forms of knowledge. Such an investigation is never primarily concerned with a pure inventory of cultural artefacts. Rather, its main concern is an analysis of the practices that produce and modify those objects, practices that provide tools and forms for the interpretation of the world.

Notes

1 For the reader of Italian, Orsi (1983) offers a comparative analysis of the two French historians on the matter.
2 The same field of research also characterized the work of Alberto Tenenti, the Italian historian most organically inserted in the French historical school (from 1965–66 he held a course on the 'social history of European cultures' at the sixth section of the École Pratique des Hautes Études).
3 Chartier also registers critiques against the paradigm of the history of mentalities put forward by Franco Venturi, Carlo Ginzburg and Geoffrey Lloyd.
4 In a book available only in Italian, Ottavia Niccoli (1979) has conducted a similar enquiry for the early modern period.
5 The experience of the encounter of Europeans with people they labelled as 'savages' also fed back to the activity of missionaries and inquisitors in the European countryside: in terms comparable to their peers overseas, they could refer to their territory as 'our own Indies' (Prosperi 1996: 551–99).
6 A similar perspective was adopted by Roche (2003) in the study of early modern spatial mobility.
7 An ambiguity of the category of identity as developed within cultural studies is denounced by Groebner (2007) in a study of the early modern forms of personal recognition and identification.
8 As an example of a cultural-historical approach (although partly *avant la lettre*), one could bring, from Italy, the critical itinerary of Piero Camporesi (1926–97), a historian of literature interested in minor authors, in the social representation of the humblest and marginal strata (the image of the

tramp), and in reading across a variety of texts to register past epochs' predominant attitudes towards the body, food, or sex. Similar topics had been explored, a generation before, by Mario Praz (1896–1982), the Italian literary critic who features most regularly among the recommended reading lists offered by French historians of mentalities (Praz 1970).

9 As further examples of what a cultural history of science looks like, one could mention Shapin and Schaffer (1985) or Galison (2003); among the historiographical reflections on the subdiscipline, Adler (2002).

10 I certainly have no intention to exaggerate the degree of idiosyncrasy in Foucault's thought and vocabulary, and I am more than happy to acknowledge the influence that, for instance, *discourse analysis* has had on sections of Anglo-Saxon academia, with resonances in Germany too (Landwehr 2008). The point I am making is that this has remained a comparatively marginal experience with respect to mainstream historical studies. Among historians who continued along some of his lines, one should also mention Arlette Farge.

4 Territories

The stages in emergence of the cultural historical perspective we examined in Chapter 2, and the research paths surveyed in Chapter 3, have partly crossed new fields of enquiry; partly gone back over familiar areas, though observing them from unusual viewpoints. Paths and territories are mutually distinguishable only to some extent, considering that a given approach will naturally be more effective in identifying and interpreting some phenomena than others. Generally speaking, all these spatial metaphors (places and itineraries) may be used as long as one bears in mind (as we stated at the beginning of Chapter 1) that what defines cultural history today – in contrast to past forms of the history of culture – is a mode of approach, rather than a specific range of objects. Once we have reaffirmed this point, the fact remains that some thematic areas and types of source have offered particularly stimulating material for the analytical models we have been describing, to the extent that they have partly come to be identified as their privileged and typical research topics.

This is not a book that specializes in enumerating types of source and suggesting fruitful ways of using them. For this purpose, the interested student or general reader will find other, dedicated resources available. Nevertheless, it is appropriate here to suggest that the fields reviewed in this chapter offer themselves for historical analysis in the form of a variety of remains – such as monuments and documents – testifying to a more distant or recent past; that texts have played a large role in shaping historical studies, and renewed approaches to texts will still be found in what follows as influential tools; however, new kinds of history have been acknowledged in part precisely for having discovered or conquered new objects: after the linguistic turn, material, pictorial (or iconic) and performative ones have been postulated. Let us briefly introduce them, before exploring some related research in further detail.

The American art historian **W. J. T. Mitchell** was one of the first theorists to suggest the notion of a pictorial turn (Mitchell 1994; Curtis 2010): the acknowledgment of the power of images and pictures, and the call for a cultural analysis capable of decoding a specific language of images, as distinguished from codes of verbal language. In what is often represented as a 'society of spectacle',[1] the life of images[2] is now examined from a variety of perspectives, and a sample of recent lines of interpretation and historical understanding will be offered below.

The case for material objects has been put in the following terms by a scholar advocating their relevance for cultural history:

> Many cultural historians ignore the physical environment in which culture is embedded. They elevate abstract ideas above things, symbolic meaning above utility, and imagination above empirical facts. They generalize from images and texts as though they were material commodities, focusing on how the world was represented and perceived, not on how it functioned or how it was physically or emotionally experienced. Style is accorded more significance than form or content; the method of representation is considered to be as meaningful as the object.
>
> (Grassby 2005: 591)

Interestingly enough, the author of the above comments pairs emotional experience with the physicality of the object, rather than with perceptions and representations: using objects – it seems – significantly involves the realm of feelings (on the latter, we will return later). With this interest in the material dimension of human life, history naturally comes close to archaeology, and expresses a curiosity for the collection, preservation and interpretation of many forms of cultural artefacts from the past. In this context, it is not surprising if, within Scandinavian academia, cultural history as a discipline derives from the renewal and merging of departments of ethnology and folklore studies (Christiansen 2008).[3] Jonas Frykman and Orvar Löfgren have offered a model example of the approach developed from this background with their perceptive analysis of the making of bourgeois culture in fin-de-siècle Sweden, focusing on the way ideas about the good and proper life 'are anchored in the routines and trivialities of everyday life [...]: in the sharing of a meal, in the structure of work, in the physical arrangement of the home' (Frykman and Löfgren 1987: 6). Consequently, we will return to material culture later in this chapter.

To texts, images and material objects, one should also add oral sources – a different foundation for historical discourse that also testifies to attitudes, feelings and forms of behaviour. Traditional, document-centred historians have been sceptical about these sources because they tend to lack precision in form or in chronology. This bias, which has lessened over the past generation, conceals the fact that oral tradition and personal reminiscence may follow a different logic and enable us to focus on particular historical phenomena: for instance, the fact that sometimes it is continuity, rather than change, that is worth exploring and demands an explanation (Prins 2001). Studies of the way and logic by which memory is individually constructed (and/or lost) also have the opportunity to take into account the findings of the neurosciences. As for the cultural construction of collective memory, it has led to the inventory and analysis of a variety of 'sites of memory' – the latter being identified either physically, as with archives and various types of buildings and spaces, or in objects such as books and monuments; or else more symbolically, in concepts and practices such as commemorations and other rituals (**Nora** 1996–98, 2001–10).[4]

In addition to the above-mentioned turns, a performative one has also been recently identified in a variety of genres of discourse within the humanities, including history (German-speaking scholars have done so overtly: see Martschukat and Patzold 2003): this is centred on a re-appreciation of the role of human agency, rather than on the exploitation of a particular type of source (although, to be accurate, the cultural, the iconic and the material too are to be intended, primarily, as different dimensions of the human experience, rather than mere families of meaningful objects). There will be a sample of this, too, in the rest of this chapter, particularly in matters of styles of reception and consumption.

In the course of the twentieth century, cultures and societies underwent transformations that have exercised manifest influences over the evolution of historiographical paradigms, from the way historians choose their topics and sources, to the patterns in which they shape their discourses. The hierarchical structure of society (in classes or orders) has obvious cultural implications: the cultural components of belonging to groups (from the basic distinction between common people and the elite), as well as the dynamics of the relationships between different groups, have themselves offered matter for pivotal studies on a variety of historical epochs and contexts.

A significant portion of such studies follow the flag of 'history from below', that is, a re-appreciation of the experience, testimony and point of view of subaltern and marginal social groups (Sharpe 2001; see also the work of **Raphael Samuel** and **Arlette Farge**). Such is the case with early modern Europe, of which Peter Burke (2009b) has identified an original popular culture, the breakaway of the (previously hardly distinguishable) privileged groups, accompanied by the implementation of forms of social control over such forms of expression; only to return, at the end of the process, via folklore studies, to a rediscovery of popular culture, by then (more or less consciously) forgotten. In turn, Burke depended on the Russian literary critic **Mikhail Bakhtin** (1984), whose notion of popular culture postulated it as antagonist to power, religious or political alike. Another example is offered by the English working class, which E. P. Thompson (1991) expressly chose to identify also by the cultural factors that characterized participation in it, against economistic reductions of the Marxist category of social class. Thompson's work is an early example and has been inspirational for a whole area of enquiry on popular culture, with particular reference to the influence of modern media, which has developed within the field of cultural studies. This was to cite just a few classic cases: obviously the entire section of historical studies that focuses on class identities would rightly fit under this headline.

Full consideration of gender as a historical factor proved even more explosive than social critique: since the first steps of the history of women, it has been questioning entrenched convictions and habits of the historical profession. Here, too, the side of cultural identities (beside that of social conditions) has opened up wide, unexplored territories of research. It would be inconceivable to ignore them today, and from this field we will start the last stage of our journey.

Gender, the family and sexuality

The histories of women and gender (Scott 2001; Kessler-Harris 2002; Meade and Wiesner-Hanks 2004; Down 2010) have vigorously imposed themselves over the past thirty years, ever since feminist movements began to orient some historical studies. Initially it was a question of conquering some space within the dominant disciplinary and professional framework: being largely a history written *by* women, as well as about them, it had to face the biases and obstacles presented by predominantly male research environments and institutions. With time, the gender perspective has become a necessary requirement for any kind of historiography aiming at being methodologically up-to-date. It may be early to declare, but one could predict that, within a foreseeable future, this perspective may disintegrate due to its own success: if it becomes unacceptable to deal with any historical phenomenon properly unless one considers its gender implications, a history of women and gender as a separate field will partly lose its raison d'être. (Similar comments were made for the case of politics by Peter Burke [2001c: 1]: 'If politics is everywhere, is there any need for political history?' – evidently, they could also apply to culture.) Naturally, this suggestion is only hypothetical, and attempts to interpret current and future trends. Also, the situation clearly varies in different countries. On this front, to continue the work already begun during the last quarter of the twentieth century, cultural battles will still need to be fought and masses of sources explored.

Both the history of women and that of gender – particularly some ground-breaking multi-author publications in the field – have paid significant attention to cultural factors, in particular to masculine and feminine models and their construction, in the conviction that naturally determined roles play a rather limited role in them. Moreover, the very opinions held by past cultures on the biological foundation of sexual difference have offered specific material for historical enquiry for more than one scholar (including Laqueur 2000). As such, the history of gender – which by definition concerns both women and men – could be defined precisely as the study of such cultural constructions of identities, as distinguished from sex, as a given biological condition. However, this would be an oversimplification of the critical debate, since influential feminist historians and theorists, such as **Joan Scott** and Judith Butler (1956–), have precisely challenged that distinction and claimed, to various degrees in their different contributions, that sex itself is a discursive construction and not a biological constraint (Scott 1988, 1999; Butler 1990, 1993). The new insights produced by the gender perspective cut across the subfields and specializations we have surveyed throughout this book, thus allowing us to address them from a different critical standpoint. For instance, a thought-provoking cultural theory of the visual, questioning vision from the viewpoint of gender difference, has been proposed by Griselda Pollock.

This development, therefore, also concerns models of masculinity: the awareness of this dimension of past experience that we recently acquired allows us to investigate it both as characteristic of given socio-cultural contexts, and as appropriated and interpreted by particular individuals. In a perspective that necessarily links social aspects (actual living conditions) and cultural aspects (world perceptions and representations), such a new gaze has overlapped with, and enriched, a line of research that, in post-war social history, had already paid significant attention to the history of the family, of the variety of its forms from the point of view of both composition and structure, and internal relationships, as well as the evolution of all these factors through time.

The history of age groups is to date comparatively less developed than that of gender and social groups. A number of studies have nevertheless researched in the areas of the history of childhood, youth and old age. As with other cases, the perspective tends to combine social and cultural aspects: on one side, the living conditions among different groups; on the other, the reconstruction of a past experience – what did it mean to be young or old in given historical circumstances? Which ideas and perceptions prevailed in the dominant attitudes towards different age groups?[5]

Philippe Ariès (1996) – whom we have encountered as a protagonist of the history of mentalities – is responsible for a reading of the history of childhood in Europe, which was epoch-making on a number of accounts:

- it was one of the first interpretations to break neatly with the idea that relationships between parents and children had no history, as if they were dictated by a kind of affection permanently rooted in the species as part of its identity;
- it was able to exploit effectively types of source that are less canonical in historical research, particularly images (where the child was traditionally represented as a miniature adult);
- it has decisively influenced the historical imagination of the general reader (to the extent that it remains commonsense knowledge, even after having proved unconvincing to a large majority of historians).

From his documentation, and from entrenched traditions such as entrusting children to wet-nurses, Ariès drew the conclusion that the model of parental love emerged only towards the end of the early modern period; up to then, in his opinion, half-hearted affection between generations had been not only the result of crude demographic circumstances (you could not invest too much emotionally in young lives that too often tended to be broken by high child mortality rates), but also partly responsible for them (you died also out of negligence).[6] As noted, this model has been the object of substantial revision, and there is no room here for a review of the responses it solicited. It remains a key historiographical reference point, at least because it testifies to the breadth and depth in the reconstruction of the past we can obtain by working on such topics. A variant in the study of age groups is offered by recent considerations of the alternating of subsequent generations as a potentially meaningful historical category that defines people living in a specific period in contrast with those that preceded and followed (Daniel 2001: 330–45; Ory 2004: 74–75).

In a way on the opposite front to Ariès – in the sense that it uncovered an unexpected presence, rather than absence, of strong feelings – was a book in which the American medievalist John Boswell (1988) wrote an absorbing page in the history of abandoned children. In a long-term overview, ranging from Greek and Roman antiquity to the threshold of early modernity, Boswell traced not a lack of affection but, on the contrary, the welcoming warmth of foster families; to the extent that, in the trust in a likely happy ending, even the choice of abandoning children lost the hard outlines of a desperate move, almost to turn into an act of parental love. This book, too, was not uncontroversial on account of the author's assembling and reading of sources, exemplified by its very title, which prominently featured a feeling (kindness), both problematic to document and disputable as a rendering of a supposedly equivalent Latin word (*misericordia* – which, however, 'glosses as compassion, mercy, or pity, all of which carry connotations of distress and the need for rescue').[7]

Boswell – a believer who campaigned in favour of the acceptation of gays and gay marriages within the Catholic Church – is also the author of a book (1980) that, in many respects, has opened the way to historical research on homosexuality. His portrait surprises the reader both in the author's estimation of the size of the phenomenon, and because it traces an ancient and high-medieval world predominantly tolerant towards same-sex love, with a turning point in the direction of intolerance dating as late as the thirteenth–fourteenth centuries. As with all works that map a brand new territory, Boswell's proposed narrative underwent significant revision with subsequent research; this, however, does not detract from his merit in having stimulated further in-depth examinations and clarifications.

One of the most striking case studies is offered by Renaissance Florence, a city at the time renowned as a heartland of sodomy, to the extent that, for most of the fifteenth century, special magistrates were appointed for its prosecution (the 'night officers'); the latter, however, did not have a reputation of being particularly strict (Rocke 1996). The way sexual behaviour was classified in contemporary perception marks this story with the attributes of a specific culture (as well as social practice): even if it was usually a question of relationships between men, what defined sodomites was not particularly the choice of their partners' gender (a factor that has only recently become decisive in qualifying one's sexual preferences), but rather the role (active, generally towards adolescents, according to a model reminiscent of the one common in ancient Greece). Moreover, Florence was not an isolated case, and Venice presented a series of similar patterns.

With these studies, we have moved to one of the most representative territories in gender history: the history of sexuality – once again, at the same time, a history of both behaviour and attitudes (dominant and marginal alike). The field has known a multiplicity of developments; here, too, the voice we cannot avoid mentioning and briefly listening to is that of Michel Foucault. As we have seen (Chapter 3), his research employed a sophisticated model of discourse analysis. Within this, the French philosopher devoted special attention to discourses concerning sexuality (Foucault 1979–88). His findings held some surprises. The Victorian age, rather than one of silence, was rediscovered as a time of the obsessive production of discourse, when virtually nothing but sex was on the agenda. Conversely, classical Greek civilization, rather than a utopian moment of free behaviour and attitudes, re-emerged from his source examination as the first step in problematizing sexual experience, which Christianity would move a step further. The early modern period took shape as the terrain of a series of experiments and fine tunings, starting from the tenacity with which confessors interrogated penitents on sexual matters, and continuing with the socio-medical concerns with monsters and the battles against masturbation (Laqueur 2003 has returned to this topic).

A premature death interrupted Foucault's (as well as Boswell's) intellectual itinerary. If, as a whole, the various historical processes his research has uncovered emphasize the importance of techniques of control and discipline of the body, it may be worth mentioning that, in explicit polemic with the Freudian theory of repression, Foucault thought primarily in terms of a development of forms of self-control by individuals; as in his previous enquiry on the history of prisons and mechanisms of justice (Foucault 1977a), the dynamics he identified – which he ultimately regarded as the background of main traits of our modern condition – went in the direction of progressively more subtle and introjected, rather than overtly oppressive, forms of social control and exercise of power. On the whole, 'what Foucault has bequeathed to historians is a history embodied' (Rubin 2002: 83). Other influential historians have moved on similar fronts: from **Peter Brown** (1988) investigating men, women and sexual renunciation in early Christianity, to **Caroline Walker Bynum** (1987) examining the religious significance of food to medieval women.

Along the boundaries with nature: the body

The history of sexuality is one area where research moves on the borderline between nature and culture, thus contributing to investigation of the very characteristics of this opposition (Serna and Pons 2005: 5–10). On this front, an important contribution came from the volume in which Keith Thomas (1983) traced human attitudes towards the natural and animal world as they developed in early modern England (as Jack Goody had the opportunity to point out, although – see Chapter 3 – from the anthropological point of view this perspective may appear faulty for lack of comparison: to be able to state that a culture has something specific, not to say unique, one needs to contrast it to a certain extent against others).

With their distinctive interest in the relationship between human beings and their surroundings, a significant number of exponents of the French historical school, from Bloch and Febvre to Braudel and Le Roy Ladurie, have contributed to the early stages of environmental history (Hughes 2006: 32–35) – a significant dimension also in American scholarship, where historians such as Frederick Jackson Turner (1861–1932; see Hughes-Warrington 2008: 367–74) emphasized the role of the western frontier on the nation's identity and imagination. Landscape was revisited by British historian **Simon Schama** (1995) in a wide-ranging perspective, which is by definition cultural since it couples its topic with memory. Among environmental conditions, climate obviously has its history too, and its cultural dimension can be fruitfully explored. The early modern scene – long pre-dating current concerns and debates over climate change – has been described as follows:

> Repentance preachers blamed the sins of humanity for the climatic vagaries of the Little Ice Age: an immediate change in behaviour would supposedly calm God's wrath and bring about better times. But the weather did not improve, even after scapegoats were identified and hunted down.
>
> (Behringer 2010: VII)

Furthermore, **Felipe Fernández-Armesto** traced nothing less than 'a brief history of humankind', a reflection on the frontier between humans and animals. He observes that recent 'arguments over the human status of Neanderthals have been conducted in terms startlingly reminiscent of nineteenth-century controversies over blacks' (Fernández-Armesto 2004: 4). And he asks in what directions the never-definitive notion of humankind may move under the influx of partially new sensitivities, such as those deriving from animal rights campaigns, or implied by such a problematic threshold as that concerning the life of the unborn child.

On this front, the exploration of sensory experience, of the way it is historically and culturally framed, is a fascinating field, one seemingly destined to openly challenge the resistance of common sense, by which we tend to regard perception and sensitivity as natural phenomena beyond the control of cultural factors. On the contrary, patterns of sight, of hearing, and their relationships with each other – the cooperation or competition between the eye and the ear, the alternating predominance of one or the other – have for some time been topics of analysis and discussion in historical anthropology, particularly engaged in this terrain when it investigates the emergence and success of different media, between orality and writing (see below in this chapter). Touch has been revisited particularly in the context of research in the history of sexuality (one could add tactility as investigated within aesthetic experience);[8] taste within a history of food that pays attention, simultaneously, to variation in habits and value systems (among many others, Fernández-Armesto (2001) has also worked on this topic). Perhaps even more original and comparatively recent is an enquiry on the story of smell, whose appearance as poor relative among the five senses may prove deceiving: a revolution in perception seems to have taken place between the mid-eighteenth and the late nineteenth centuries, by which odours were discovered and social practices put into action to cancel their effects (Corbin 1986, see also 1995). A narrative of the evolution of our sensorial universe as a whole has proposed a general three-step chronology: a traditional sensorial order, which lasted from antiquity to the early modern period, marked by the aforementioned hierarchies and enriched by a whole repertory of allegories; an eighteenth–nineteenth-century passage from the world of senses to that of reason, characterized by the motif of the education of the senses and the birth of aesthetics, that is, of a new notion of taste; lastly, a twentieth-century rediscovery of senses accompanied, among other features, by the exploration of extra-sensorial perception (Jütte 2004; see also Classen 1993; Smith 2007).

Passions or emotions typically represent those aspects of human experience we used to place predominantly in the sphere of nature (therefore within the realm of the unchanging, or nearly so, almost without history by definition). On the contrary, recent critical orientations have claimed them for the territory of the historian, particularly as an effect of the growing impulse to emphasize the socially and culturally constructed aspects of human experience and agency – that is, historically determined conditions, which vary from one culture to another. From this perspective, emotions have an actual social history, a history, that is, of life experiences (not just of their cultural reflections and representations). This was already programmatically suggested by Lucien Febvre, in a wellknown essay he published during World War II. While acknowledging that 'they may well arise in the organic structure proper to a certain individual', he observed that 'they imply relations between one man and another – group relations'. Therefore, 'the emotions became a sort of *institution*. They were controlled in the same way as a ritual' (Burke 1973: 14–15).

However, the paradigm so far dominant in analysing them has been subject to recent criticism. An American specialist, Barbara Rosenwein (2002), has labelled it a 'hydraulic model', by which unrestrained passions are understood to naturally boil over in a human being who is still at an infantile, not wholly civilized stage; while the challenge of modernity would appear as a more or less successful effort in controlling them. This anthropological model, which lists Freudian psychoanalysis among its possible variants, forms the grounds for a variety of historical narratives (different as they may be from one another in other respects): on one side such representations of medieval humans as that (rather speculative) by Huizinga; on another, stories of a civilizing process that, in the same epoch, is supposed to have started in Europe (in particular according to the influential historical sociology of Norbert Elias; see below). In contrast, more recent studies have emphasized how much, say, a burst of anger or a rush of affection might have been, even in a comparatively remote past, natural only to a little degree, socially and culturally constructed to a much larger one. As a result, historical processes of change in this area would not vanish; they would, rather, multiply and acquire additional complexity. These reasons combined make the present field of enquiry exciting and expanding.

A research itinerary that has produced a significant wealth of studies in this region is that undertaken by the American historian **Peter Stearns**, the author, over a quarter of a century, of various books and collaborative works. He has explored such topics as anger and jealousy, and the dynamics of self-control in the experience of modern North Americans. He also discussed a variety of potential explanations of the historical development of emotions, ranging from their recognition as a by-product of wider social change, to the crediting of a more significant autonomy. **Theodore Zeldin** has also worked on this frontier, both on nineteenth-century France and from a wider geographical and chronological perspective.

This area of study requires detailed examination of the historical vocabulary, from the terms describing particular feelings to more general categories: at both ends of the spectrum, a variety of words have been in use that can only partially count as synonyms. According to one of the most influential accounts of this historical development, over the eighteenth and nineteenth centuries, secularization produced a move from a predominantly moral perception to a neutral, scientific framework: from passions to emotions (Dixon 2003). Since a vocabulary and set of attitudes is shared, and particular groups may be character- ized by specific norms of emotional valuation and expression, a notion of 'emotional community' has been introduced (Rosenwein 2006), with the idea that different communities coexisted, and some were dominant at times.

In turn, William Reddy (2001) has observed that, today, the majority of historical studies take for granted that what is accessible to us are only representations of emotions, rather than emotions actually experienced. On the contrary, he has suggested as desirable and attainable – partly thanks to information made available today by cognitive psychology and anthropology – a retrieval of emotional regimes of the past, which were not just conceptual categories, but allowed individuals who adopted them to actually feel in different ways. As an example, he cites the Swiss literary figure Madame de Staël (1766–1817), who thought novels made it possible for their readers to actually experience different, more nuanced feelings.

It has even been suggested that, in today's climate of scepticism over the possibility of narrating events as they really happened, what we are really able to do is almost exclusively to register what impression it made, how people felt while participating or assisting in such events: to be honest, a large part of our sources pay witness to precisely this (Fernández-Armesto 2002). The statement is a deliberately provoking one if we bear in mind that the nineteenth-century model of academic historiography (commonly labelled as 'positivist'), as exemplified by and modelled on the work of Leopold von Ranke (1795–1886), expected the discipline to be based on the collecting and publishing of source material and was based on the presupposition that documents gave us objective access to facts 'as they really happened', free of any adulterating subjective factor (Ranke 2010).

Altogether, these approaches have recently come to form the 'adventures of the body' – as Bloch defined them in the 1930s, when he claimed a space for them within historical narrative. Half a century later, Aline Rousselle – the author of a key study of early Christianity and its attitudes in matters of sexuality – could write that historians had not arrived at this field on their own initiative, but under the stimulus of a series of research paths initiated outside the discipline: 'history of disease written by physicians, of torture by solicitors, of the female body, after Simone de Beauvoir, by women, of initiations and healing by ethnographers' (Rousselle 1986: 156). However, a few years later, Roy Porter (2001, originally published in 1991) – one of the most original and prolific practitioners of the social history of medicine (1946–2002) – believed he could register a 'resurrection' of the body in scholarship.

A good example of the features of this kind of history is offered by the collective work produced by a French publisher (Corbin *et al.* 2005–06). To obtain an idea of the field of study as it has recently taken shape, one can consider the itineraries by which the editors of the three volumes arrived at this initiative, which aims at producing a preliminary work of synthesis. Georges Vigarello has explored the notions of clean versus dirty, healthy versus unhealthy, the history of gymnastics and sport – seen as the terrain of a physical taming of individuals – as well as sexual violence or the changing canons of beauty. **Alain Corbin** (referred to above) is the author of pioneering studies of odours and sensitivity. Jean-Jacques Courtine co-authored a study of the history of the face – that is of how, between the sixteenth and nineteenth centuries, emotions have been expressed or else concealed (Courtine and Haroche 1994) – and has subsequently studied the story of the public exhibition of human monsters. A work of comparable scope and dimensions has subsequently appeared in English (Kalof and Bynum 2010 – as stated within the Series preface, a publication programmatically devoted to 'reviewing the changing cultural construction of the human body throughout history').

Several of these topics also manifestly display aspects of social history: it is clearly a question of body *practices*, which in each historical context have invested the psychophysical being of the individuals involved. Nevertheless, the cultural side is present to a significant degree: the element of a *construction* of a social identity is strongly perceivable, to the extent that the phrase 'the invention of the body' has become not infrequent today. At first sight paradoxical, and certainly deliberately provoking, the expression is not, however, particularly bizarre, and fits in a now-extended family of similar cases, which opened up in the 1980s when a group of historians published a collective volume famously (and once more, ahead of subsequent imitations, provocatively) entitled *The Invention of Tradition*. In it, they were emphasizing how recent was the origin of a number of rituals and customs that are presented as traditional and seem to suggest much further distant roots that the ones they actually have (Hobsbawm and Ranger 1983).[9]

Similarly, from their very title, a couple of French books have talked in terms of an 'invention' of the body. One, by Nadeije Laneyrie-Dagen (1997), is engaged in retrieving a particular sensitivity to the physical specificity of human beings, which seems to characterize Western art (to begin with, the opacity of shade-casting figures). The other examines the 'specific manner of perceiving and capturing the nature, structure and functioning of the human body' that was imposed with the sixteenth-century rise of anatomical practice (Mandressi 2003: 12). The sectioning of corpses was not an obvious and natural option, one which only had to wait for the abandoning of taboos and prohibitions; the need to penetrate the body to reveal its mysteries, the simple fact that this was conceivable, needs to be understood in its historical surfacing as the product of a shift in mentalities. On the whole, as Corbin suggests in the introduction to the volume of the *Histoire du corps* concerning the nineteenth century,

> the body is a fiction, a cluster of mental representations, an unconscious image that is elaborated, dissolved and reconstructed along the line of the history of the individual, through the mediation of social discourse and symbolic systems.
>
> (Corbin *et al.* 2005–06, Vol. II: 9)

Material culture and consumption

As **John Brewer** (2004: 7) wrote:

> Over the past forty years, historiography has made of 'daily life' – of the experiences, actions and habits of ordinary people – a legitimate object of historical enquiry. The new social history, the history written within the framework of the recent movements centred on the topics of gender, race and sexual orientation, *Alltagsgeschichte* [history of everyday life] in Germany, microhistory in Italy and post-*Annales* cultural history in France, concentrate on the intimate, the personal, the emotional, the small-scale perspective, the everyday, the ordinary.

In carrying out such a research programme, the aforementioned orientations:

- have contrasted abstract social theorizing, as practised by structuralism and economistic Marxism, by emphasizing, on the contrary, the importance of experience;
- have distanced themselves from grand historical narratives, centred on the economic processes of modernization and political processes of liberalization, with their tendency to employ 'a unique model of

time, linear and progressive, by which all societies are measured'
(Brewer 2004: 11) – the old and by now unacceptable theory of the
stages in the development of societies, according to which there is
one and only path towards wealth and democracy, and a set yardstick
allows us to assess at which stage of evolution each given human
community has arrived at any given time;

• have given more attention to subjectivity, to everyday human
  agency, for which French theorist Michel de Certeau has proposed
  some of the most thought-provoking analyses – the latter include
  techniques according to which individuals are able to exploit
  circumstances and dodge forms of power and control (*ibid.*).

There are, predictably, various precedents in the study of the history
of everyday life, and along these lines **Jurij Lotman** provided insightful
revisitations of the culture of eighteenth-century Russia, which surveyed
such practices as dance, card play, the duel, courtship, marriage and
divorce (Lotman 1997). In the German-speaking area, *Alltagsgeschichte*
has developed as a movement particularly engaged in studying the
everyday reality of ordinary people in specific communities, with a
distinctive interest in exploring local life conditions of Germans at the
time of Nazism – in truth in a predominantly social, rather than cultural,
perspective (**Lüdtke** 1995; Daniel 2001: 298–313).

These orientations were influenced by the historical sociology of
Norbert Elias: developed in intellectual isolation several decades
before, the latter worked internationally as one of the most widespread
sources of inspiration for historical research, particularly in the 1980s.
At its heart was the idea of a civilizing process, which includes a
shifting threshold in the control of instincts. It thus offered a model
reconstruction of the foundations of power relationships, which
allowed accounting for the circumstances of the historical development
of the exercise of power on individuals. This operated as a parallel
description to Foucault's wellknown analyses of the birth of the prison
and, generally, the rise of new forms of social discipline. In this context, Elias's studies emphasized the spread of manners, as well as the
ritual games that regulated social relationships within the environment
of the court (Elias 1994, 2006).

The dynamics of sports violence also featured among the topics of
research explored by Elias. Together with his British colleague Eric
Dunning, the German sociologist interpreted them in the light of the
same model of a civilizing process, with the domestication of previously
more warlike forms of competition and physical confrontation, progressively softened and regulated (Elias and Dunning 1986). Considering

the particular status play has within the sphere of social practice, it is interesting to note a specific paragraph on play as a characteristic research field within one of the overviews of current cultural history (Ory 2004: 92–95).

Play and leisure are indeed a highly significant area of sociability – a particularly relevant one for specific social and age groups, such as youths. It is a field of enquiry for which social history has put forward important research tools, as in the case of the whole reflection on matters of ritual. The most influential interpretation of this sphere of behaviour, and of the cultural attitudes that accompany and characterize such behaviour, was offered by Mikhail Bakhtin (1984), with his interpretation of medieval and Renaissance laughter, carnival and popular culture as background to Rabelais's creative writing (a critical view of his approach has been offered by, among others, **Aron J. Gurevich**).[10]

As we have suggested (Chapter 1), ritual is one of the areas in which historians had the most fruitful opportunities to benefit from the categories devised, and the research carried out, by anthropologists. The study of such fields as religion and politics, analysed from the point of view of the ritual practice they imply, and which they embody, has produced a significant amount of scholarship. The American historian Edward Muir (2005) – a specialist, in particular, in the public ritual of the early modern Republic of Venice – has also revisited in an authoritative volume the nature and function of the whole European ritual system. According to his reconstruction, the Reformation represented an epoch of ritual crisis or revolution. Until then, a variety of rituals were accredited with the power to produce effects automatically by the mere fact of being performed. It could even happen that the wrong heir to the throne may be crowned, or people's roles were exchanged within other ceremonies: the latter would nevertheless maintain their efficacy. Once the expected words were pronounced and the gesture performed, the receivers were invested with their new roles. After that historical turning point, however, such efficacy significantly declined, and ceremonial formulae were reduced to 'mere ritual' – by definition an insufficient and inessential ground for the legitimacy of acts and titles. This framework may also prove a fruitful setting for the research that has been carried out on gesture and the cultural codes governing the meaning it socially attracted (Bremmer and Roodenburg 1991; Schmitt 1990 offers a survey of the medieval period).

Even a consideration of the objects of everyday use, recommended by both a wide notion of culture and an attention to the forms of daily life, is positioned at the crossroads between social and cultural history. On one side, it is a question of drawing up a typology of material objects and their uses, making their inventories and studying their archaeology, following their stories between permanence, material modifications and metamorphoses of usage. At the same time, all this is also highly relevant for a mapping of continuity and change in human needs, sensitivity, taste and habits – thus adding a cultural perspective to the already existing technological, economic and social ones. The different sides of this narrative are hardly distinguishable.

Among the historians who have worked at this kind of inventory, **Daniel Roche** (1994, 2000) deserves special mention as a model for the historical analysis of *material culture*, including clothing, food and technology (Pesez 1988).[11] Carlo M. Cipolla (1965, 1967) had already worked in the perspective of a history of material culture, at the cross-roads between technology, society and culture: on cannons and sails, as well as clocks (on the latter, but at the time of modern industrialization, their diffusion and its relation with the imposing of disciplined labour, see Thompson 1991). So did a pupil of Elias, Johan Goudsblom (1992), in his chronologically wide study of fire and its influence on civilization. A team of art historians and historians of science, who met a few years ago at the Max Planck Institute in Berlin, proposed an intriguing analysis of a sample of objects – from the curiosities that fill Hieronymus Bosch's paintings to soap bubbles. They tried to avoid both the extremes of considering them either as signifiers awaiting for a meaning that only a specific culture can give them, or as purely determined by their material features. They precisely aimed at reconstructing the interface between such two planes: how things 'talk', from their very physical being but also in the context of a universe of meanings, which directly concerns them (Daston 2004).

In a series of radio programmes broadcast by the BBC in 2010, *A History of the World*, the Director of the British Museum Neil McGregor took 100 objects from the museum's collection, dating from 2 million years ago to the present day and geographically spanning the planet, thus ranging from flint to mobile phone, as examples of what a rich history of humanity can be told through the objects we have made. The series also offered a good example of the communicative potentials of multimediality, with deep zoom imagery and short videos of the objects available on the programme's web site. (It also testified how valuable museums can be for research and education in cultural history.)

In this area, we should not lose sight of the specific sphere of cultural consumption. John Brewer (1997) offers a valuable example in the case of eighteenth-century England, with its characteristic spaces, a novelty in comparison with the earlier primacy of the court: from coffee houses, to reading societies and cultural clubs, to pleasure gardens. In general, emphasis on the side of consumption, rather than production, has been characteristic of recent developments in economic history, itself a discipline that has been informed by the cultural aspects of the process of material reproduction in the societies examined. Studies in this field have allowed us to anticipate the dating of a social behaviour, previously largely regarded as a consequence of transformations in the production process. A commercial revolution, or even the rise of an early consumer society, is now considered as a development already in place in seventeenth-century Europe, ahead of the eighteenth-century restructuring of manufacture, from which the modern factory was generated. The study of shopping habits, of the market behaviour of different agents, changes in taste and the importance of gender are now fully considered, and help depict lively portraits, as Evelyn Welch (2005) has done for the shopping habits inaugurated during the Renaissance.

On the other hand, sale did not hold any monopoly among the forms of exchange of goods in early modern Europe. It cohabited with two different relational models: coercion and gift. The research orientation known as 'economic anthropology' (exemplified at its best by the work of Karl Polanyi) chiefly emphasized precisely that the market logic is not the only one around, and it established its supremacy in specific historical conditions. In particular, the gift is a dimension on which, in the 1920s, the French sociologist and anthropologist Marcel Mauss wrote key comments, not short of nostalgia for that model of human relationships. However, when Natalie Zemon Davis studied the case of the French sixteenth century, one of her points was to depart from a narrative of a one-way evolution from a pre-modern economy based on the gift to a modern one centred on the market. She argued convincingly that 'gift exchange persists as an essential relational mode, a repertoire of behavior, a register with its own rules, language, etiquette, and gestures' (Davis 2000: 14–15).

Both Welch's Renaissance shopping habits and Roche's world of eighteenth-century Parisian fashion shed light on the culture of clothing, a subject with a rich anthropological background and resonance. On this front, fresh information and ideas have come from the research conducted – again on the Renaissance, with focus on Germany – by Ulinka Rublack. It shows what importance people from the past – across the spectrum of social hierarchy, contrary to the dominant assumption that the poor always wore rags – conferred on the choice of what to wear, the meanings they attributed to appearance and the ways this influenced how they felt and moved. It also bears witness to the way in which people's greater involvement with such objects 'was related to a new visual culture and mediality, a whole set of visual practices, and a greater status given to visual perception' (Rublack 2010: 21).

The influential analyses put forward by Certeau (evoked by Brewer, above), both as a theorist and as a practising historian, provided the most comprehensive and thought-provoking reflection on this whole range of daily practices:

> The repetitive routines of our life and work that we largely take for granted – such as walking and sauntering, eating and consuming, getting dressed and going out, greeting, touching, playing, remembering, telling, and chatting – are for Certeau clues as to how individual people shape culture. They testify to the *tactics* they employ in order to appropriate a personal or group-related living space and invest it with their own meaning. This takes place in an environment offered to them as a strategic 'concept' from above or from the outside by the institutions that wield power, such as the state, the community, the business world, or any number of other intermediary corporations. People accept those institutions as conditions and frameworks for their action, but – in what Certeau calls the 'symbolism of the unconscious' – they then follow their own course, at times in direct opposition to what is offered by the official, 'utopian' programming. They 'poach' on the territory of others in order to realize their own culture.
>
> (Frijhoff 2010: 84; see Certeau 1984)

Media and communication

In one respect, the book is one of the consumer goods we have just discussed: therefore it is with some connection with the history of material culture that the history of the book – of its metamorphoses, its social usages – has been eloquently developed and enriched over the past few decades. What makes this territory utterly special, though, is the fact that, for millennia, writing and reading have represented by far the chief means of elaboration and transmission of cultural identities; consequently, this role of theirs – and their changing relations on one side with orality, on the other with images – has imposed itself as a decisive area of reflection, at the crossroads of a variety of different disciplinary fields (sociological, psychological and linguistic). It is thus a crucial ground for cultural history: in a way, it is a metahistorical dimension – a cultural history of cultural history – because the limits, forms and operating of the production and circulation of culture provide its very objects.

Significantly, on this front some of the most remarkable pages in our history have been written, and some ongoing debates opened. Here, too, clearly in the wake of momentous change presently under way, this perspective has forced itself as an aspect of the evolution of social relations, one that can no longer be ignored (Briggs and Burke 2005) and presents significant implications for the political sphere (the public sphere on which the German theorist Jürgen Habermas has written wellknown reflections). Just as we have encountered London coffee houses as sites of cultural consumption, their Paris equivalents offered the focus of the address which Robert Darnton gave in 1999 as President of the American Historical Association. The paper – subsequently published online, in an experimental format that included images, interactive maps and original songs, as if inaugurating a new frontier in communication in the humanities – introduces coffee houses as a vehicle of an 'early information society', meeting points which the police kept under strict surveillance, to collect information on the political activity that took place in them (Darnton 2000).

The study that, in many respects, originated the full modern acknowledgement of the impact of the media, also did so with reference to the present and the audio-visual revolutions in the twentieth-century communication system. In *The Gutenberg Galaxy: The making of typographic man* (McLuhan 1962), the Canadian literary critic Herbert Marshall McLuhan (1911–80) suggested from his very subtitle a deep, epoch-making transformation. Among other theses, it included the debated attribution of forms of perception and graphic-artistic convention to social construction. The case of the Renaissance invention of linear perspective aptly illustrates the issue: is it a particularly efficacious and realistic imitation of three-dimensionality, or else a purely pictorial convention, an arbitrary code of representation, comparable with, and not necessarily superior to, others? *The Gutenberg Galaxy* emphasized without hesitation the conventional and culturally specific nature of perspective; in so doing, it had been preceded by a pioneering study by Erwin Panofsky (1991) who had interpreted it 'as symbolic form'. McLuhan also observed that conventions concerning representation in film, taken for granted in Western culture, were anything but natural: from the rhetorical codes that regulate the selection and juxtaposition of images in a sequence, to the presupposition of the spectator's passivity; to the extent that their assimilation by people not previously exposed to them requires some training. The long-term dynamic suggested a transition from the supremacy of the ear to that of the eye, marked by such key shifts as that from orality to reading (with the internalizing of phonetic alphabet), through the manuscript culture of the Middle Ages, up to the typographic revolution. To the latter he ascribed not only direct consequences – for instance, a reader's mental frame dominated by the standardized nature of the printed word and page – but also a staggering list of further repercussions: from turning change, as technological progress, into the very norm of social life, to providing, in the printed page, a substitute for auricular confession.

McLuhan was not an isolated figure. He belonged to what is known as the Toronto School of Communication – a vein of study that began in the 1950s and proposed a pioneering reflection on the matter, as a result of a multiplicity of disciplinary approaches: from the study by the economist Harold Innis (1894–1952) on the implications, over millennia, of technological options chosen within the field of communication (with such transitions as writing on paper rather than stone), to Eric Havelock's (1903–88) and Walter Ong's (1912–2003) research on orality and writing from the ancient Greeks onwards (Havelock 1986; Briggs and Burke 2005). *The Gutenberg Galaxy* is a deliberately provocative volume in its tone and radical in its theses, which inevitably attracted polemic reaction and suggested less schematic and more nuanced reconstructions. McLuhan's neat contrast between the manuscript and the printed book has variously been corrected by pointing at their similarities, elements of continuity and mixed forms (that is, the frequent coexistence of printed and handwritten parts within the same books, if not even the same pages). The sheer dimensions of the manuscript circulation of texts, as it survived at least until the eighteenth century, has prompted scholars to speak of 'scribal publication' – a notion that has been applied, for instance, to describe the production of texts in seventeenth-century England or in Renaissance Italy (Love 1993; Richardson 2009).[12]

Half a century later, we know the history of the book and of reading in much more detail. It is interesting to note that the best known and accepted synthetic assessment of the historical impact the introduction of the printing press had on modern culture and society (**Eisenstein** 1979, 1993) to a large extent re-proposed, in a more moderate version, McLuhan's thesis on discontinuity. Among the contributions to this field of enquiry, an influential one has been offered by the Italian palaeographer **Armando Petrucci**, a scholar concerned with the diffusion and social role of writing, specialist in the written sources of medieval Italy, aware not only of the more strictly technical characteristics of written documents, but also of the material aspects of the circulation of texts (as in the case of pocket-books, whose portability defined their role while assigning them a defined and significantly wide public).

In comparison with the systematic studies in the history of the book and of publishing that were undertaken in France during the first decades of the post-war period, the following scenario of research registered a shift that gave readers and modes of reading centre stage, an example of a wider tendency to move from an earlier emphasis on cultural products to a new one on cultural practice. A protagonist of such orientation is Roger Chartier, a cultural historian who – also benefiting from **Pierre Bourdieu**'s sociology of cultural production[13] – has been engaged for some time on the fronts of both original research and methodological reflection. Chartier has developed the notion of communities of readers characterized by shared practices, and, following interpretive paths opened up by Michel de Certeau, emphasized the creativeness of readers' appropriation of texts (Chartier 1994); he has paid attention to the material form of production and circulation of texts, and their contextual influences (for instance, the constraint deriving from patronage: Chartier 1995); he has rediscovered materials, from wax tablets to small notebooks, on which texts were written not in order to last, but to be erased and leave room to others (Chartier 2007). Among his numerous contributions, one could single out his attention to the modes of reading and the forms of sociability that have historically been associated with them. For instance, reading aloud is also documented for the early modern period, thus correcting the impression that it had progressively been replaced by silent reading:[14] the two forms seem, instead, to have coexisted for a long time and satisfied different needs. In fact, forms of loud reading have played a significant role in circulating a variety of texts (sometimes specifically produced for that destination) beyond the circle of active readers. Furthermore, on the interaction between the oral and the written, the French historian has offered documentation by examining the theatrical literature of early modern Europe: the transfer of texts from the scene to the page and vice versa, as well as the weight their graphic layout on the printed page played in their reception (Chartier 1999b). In examining these details, Chartier had the opportunity to benefit both from a reflection on graphic culture as proposed by Petrucci, and from the Anglo-Saxon tradition of analytical bibliography.

A key contribution in shaping subsequent studies on the history of the book – such historians as Darnton and Chartier have made comprehensive use of it – has come particularly from the research of New Zealand bibliographer Donald McKenzie (1931–99), ever since his 1960s enquiries on the work practices of seventeenth-century

English publishing. For the model of knowledge he has proposed since the 1970s, McKenzie coined the term 'sociology of texts'.

The methodological proposal consists in taking into full consideration the fact that the text, rather than being 'authorially sanctioned, contained, and historically definable' is 'always incomplete, and therefore open, unstable, subject to a perpetual re-making by its readers, performers, or audience' (McKenzie 1999: 55).[15] His experience as typographer and the competence as bibliographer allowed the New Zealand scholar to cross the border between a philology interested only in the verbal content of texts, and a bibliography confined to registering seemingly extra-textual details: his analyses made it possible to appreciate the role played by such details as punctuation or typos in the interpretation (and in the misunderstanding) of texts. They also led him to identify the contribution of individual typesetters (and of their linguistic habits) in the fixing of the text of classics of English drama (similarly, Richardson [1994] reconstructed how the text of the classics of Italian fourteenth-century literature – Dante, Petrarch and Boccaccio – as we know it today, is the product of sixteenth-century printing enterprises). As an example of the influence the shape of a text may have upon the reader (as we saw, one of McLuhan's key themes), McKenzie mentions that, at the turn of the eighteenth century, the English philosopher John Locke criticized the effects of the graphic presentation of the text of the Bible as articulated in chapter and verse. According to Locke, such structure encouraged the use of the Scripture as if it were a collection of independent aphorisms, thus breaking up the thread of the discourse of accomplished works such as the letters of Paul the apostle; and ended up facilitating an instrumental use of biblical quotes as a simple means to justify predetermined positions, rather than a reading experience that encourages meditation.

In a series of conferences held in 1985 at the British Library, McKenzie also proposed an extension of the notion of text, which should include such 'non-book texts' as maps, films and disc recordings. His proposal could seem to be in tune with the critical orientation, influenced by the postmodern condition and the *linguistic turn* (see Chapter 2), to interpret everything as text, to the extent of blurring any distinction between history and fiction and abandoning the need to refer a text to an external realm (a context), in which the text would have to be put to be correctly understood. On the contrary, McKenzie (1999, 2002) valued both the historical context and the role played by archival documents. His recommendation may also prove valuable in reminding us to what extent the book form – which dominated recent experience of reading until the latest boom in word processing and the electronic transmission of texts – was in the past only one of the available formats, and readers had wide and frequent experience of different forms of writing, such as those on sheets or separate leaves.

One should also add that this discipline is no arid bibliography: it can allow the full recovery of the historical momentum of events that have exercised significant weight on the life experience of thousands of human beings. An example is offered by the case of the Treaty of Waitangi, by which, in its interpretation by colonial authorities, in 1840 some forty Maori chiefs ceded their lands to the British Crown. McKenzie's reflections on the cultural exchange that was behind this document are summarized by the editors of a collection of his essays as follows:

> Exposing the gulf between an imperial culture, which privileged the written word, and the native oral culture, McKenzie revealed how both parties brought contradictory understandings of writing and its authority to the agreement they signed. For the Maori, who had lived with scribal and printed texts – imposed by the British – for just twenty years, genuinely binding pledges and promises could be made only orally, in accordance with long-established traditions. For the colonizers, however, the act of signing a written document alone conferred legal authority.
>
> (McKenzie 2002: 8)

Anthropology adds a further, essential dimension to the study of media and of their impact on individuals and social groups, thanks to the discipline's theoretical insights and the clues emerging from the comparison between different cultures. British social anthropologist Jack Goody has been sensitive to the impact literacy is having on those less developed cultures – particularly, in today's Africa – that have experienced only recent direct contact with the Western world (as the Maori did a century earlier), and therefore, since the 1960s, he has assigned literacy a key role in processes of modernization. On the other hand, this appreciation has not offered further fuel to a doctrine of the uniqueness of the European experience; on the contrary, it has allowed a substantial revision and relocation of it within a wider perspective. On one side, Goody moves the invention of writing – a key shift, given the role played by its logic in shaping the structure of society – backwards from the Greeks to the civilizations of the ancient Near East (Mesopotamia and Egypt): in that area, the use of writing was responsible for the diffusion of religions (in one way or another, all religions of the book), the rise of literate elites exercising social hegemony, the formation of political structures equipped with coherent legal systems, as well as the development of a complex economy capable of using techniques of accounting. On the other hand, if such effects are not a monopoly of alphabetic writing alone, the role played by literacy in the experience of the ancient civilization of the Far East also needs reconsidering (Goody 1977, 1986). This interpretation does not consider writing in isolation: on the contrary, it regards orality as a ubiquitous form of human communication: the latter, therefore, is either oral only, or oral and written; and, in the second case, displays a series of forms of interplay between the two dimensions: from the relations orality and writing entertain within one and the same individual, to those displayed within a given society, or between societies of differing degree or type of literacy.

Furthermore, slightly diminishing the importance played by alphabetic writing, Goody's research appreciated forms of writing other than the representation of discourse, as the case of lists exemplifies; and suggests the ways they may have influenced modes of thought. The earliest writing systems already allowed the compilation of lists, giving names in separate and abstract form, therefore remote from oral speech. This is the case of:

- retrospective lists, 'a kind of inventory of persons, objects or events' as administrative lists, which led to the development of registers;
- 'the shopping list, which serves as a guide for future action, a plan. Items get struck off, mentally or physically, as they are dealt with. One example that is currently found among systems of restricted literacy in West Africa as well as in early writing systems in the Middle East, is the itinerary used, for example, to map out the route an individual has to take on the pilgrimage to Mecca' (Goody 1977: 80);
- lexical lists – for instance, in Mesopotamia, 'a kind of inventory of concepts, a proto-dictionary or embryonic encyclopaedia' (ibid.)

On the whole, this perspective of enquiry attributes to media a privileged role, formerly assigned to structures of production or forms of authority.

The above-mentioned widening of the notion of text also involves attention to elements and aspects of a book that at first glance would appear marginal, such as its frontispiece, format and dedications – the apparatus that has taken the collective name of *paratext*. Footnotes – a tool which, by editorial choice, is used sparingly within the present book – have been the object of a monographic study, in a reconstruction that also vividly portrays national variations in the style of annotation

(Grafton 1997). It tells a story with various and far away roots. A central episode is occupied by the work of Leopold von Ranke, a German scholar who, in the first half of the nineteenth century, invented modern historiography as an academic discipline by centring it in the collecting and editing of primary sources (even if in a partly contradictory way: precisely the historian who exalted the importance of sources seems to have been personally inconsistent, if not inaccurate, in citing them).

The account is particularly meaningful because it is set at the crossroads between:

* the history of the different manners in which, through time, research has been conducted; and
* that of the literary form taken on each occasion by the publication of its results.

Such an interweaving is highly significant at times, like ours, when the distinction between history and fiction has been the object of close scrutiny, and has even been put into question. To tell the truth, this is a revival of an old challenge, if one considers that the model of the discipline which Ranke founded was precisely intended to differentiate history writing from the historical novel (at the time of Walter Scott's literary fortune).

The story of writing and reading is obviously related to patterns of literacy, cultural practices of individual and social memory, processes of formation of identity: all this has attracted significant scholarly interest on what we can learn from egodocuments (autobiographical writing in a loose sense and in a variety of forms) and the writing of ordinary people – as in the case of Jacques-Louis Ménétra (1986), the artisan studied by Daniel Roche; or of Johan Hjerpe, the industrious artisan from eighteenth-century Stockholm studied by Arne Jarrick (1999).[16] James Amelang has followed this research path with particular determination, first by studying the diary of Miquel Parets, a seventeenth-century tanner from Barcelona, and moving subsequently to a wide-ranging enquiry on early modern European artisan autobiography (Amelang 1998). His focus is on the practice of writing rather than on its products, with the aim ultimately to understand the motives behind popular writing, something the authors appear to have found close to their heart and identity (paraphrasing Descartes, Amelang has his typical diarist stating 'I write, therefore I am'). Such a little-known background may also allow seeing literary masterpieces like Jean-Jacques Rousseau's *Confessions* as the tip of an iceberg with some relations with contemporary culture, and not simply as the result of an isolated, revolutionary genius.

Reading images

The aforementioned expansion of the spectrum of sources is even more visible with the case of the full consideration of images – including the most obvious addition comparable and related to literary texts, that is, the artistic tradition (Poirrier 2004: 291–320). In the study of iconographic material, different approaches converge, from an intellectual tradition such as that associated with the Warburg Institute (see Chapter 2) to new perspectives in cultural history, as exemplified by the reconsideration of the role played by images in religious propaganda in the age of the Reformation, a reconsideration begun by **Robert Scribner** (1994), with critical results that have profoundly rewritten the history of that crucial page in European history.

A mature reflection on this type of source requires full awareness of at least two aspects of the story: on one side, what uses individuals and institutions from the past made of images; on the other side, to what features and dimensions of past worlds we can gain access today through visual evidence, what it allows us to reconstruct and what it does not (Gaskell 2001; Burke 2001a, 2010a). It is a question, among other tasks, of recovering the perceptual structures and cultural frameworks within which contemporaries themselves set their own visual experiences. This was noted some time ago by Chartier (1986: 347):

> As with texts, attention is diverted from the analysis, serial or not, of iconographic materials, to capture their uses and interpretations. A (difficult) history of the ways of reading the image is thus outlined, one set at the crossroads between a historical sociology of systems of perception and the making conventions explicit, inscribed in the work and (more or less) known to the producer and the onlookers. The image is, therefore, apprehended as a historical document whose technical, stylistic, iconographic properties refer to a particular mode of perceiving, a manner of seeing moulded by social experience, and engaged in the reading of the painting, the engraving or the statue. Precisely this manner of seeing becomes the primary object of research, explored, or rather seized in the comparison between codes and conventions of figurative representations and different traces of the schemes of perception proper of a given epoch.

The example Chartier gave to document this approach is highly representative. It is a masterful study of the vocabulary and the conceptual frame by which fifteenth-century Italian culture spoke of contemporary art. It identifies the humanists' grammar and rhetoric as engaged in an observation of art which strongly influenced the period's taste and contributed to the discovery of pictorial composition. The heir of a 100-year-old iconographic tradition, the art historian who has authored this research, **Michael Baxandall** (1971, 1988), taught at the Warburg Institute and is responsible for an original reinterpretation of an epoch's 'period eye', which abandons a purely stylistic reading of the work of art isolated from its social and cultural context, and returns the artists' choices to the circumstances that defined and qualified them, thus at the same time better appreciating the active role played by the public and by those who had commissioned the work. His model of analysis has been the object of some criticism, comparable with the critiques addressed to the history of mentalities, as if it left limited room for the coexistence of different groups, each with their own codes for viewing (Bryson 1992); in the context of these historical analyses and debates, a wider and more complex notion of *visual culture* has been introduced over the past few decades – an expression which the American art historian Svetlana Alpers (who co-chaired with Greenblatt the founding editorial board of *Representations*) credited to Baxandall.

The visual culture dominant in early modern Europe was the subject of a thorough enquiry by Stuart Clark (2007), who has assembled convincing documentation proving the uncertain reliability that sight was assigned in a variety of fields – from art theory to science and religion – during an epoch in search of the real, troubled by notions of deception and illusion, and thus prone to questioning the function of images as well as the authenticity of visions, notwithstanding the centrality of the eye in Western culture. This can be seen as a further development of a perspective that was already present in the work of David Freedberg (1989) on psychological responses to art: from Christian attitudes to the representation of sacred personages and the miracles attributed to them, to the role of effigies in legal practice or hostile reactions to images, including censorship and iconoclasm.

The references we have encountered throughout this book to images as specific historical sources, to sight as a sense with a history of its own, or appearance as the terrain of particular cultural practices (as in the case of clothing), all converge to suggest a growing status and interest for the visual in the historical imagination of our own time. The study of visual culture (or *visual studies*) has emerged from the late 1980s as an interdisciplinary field 'for the study of the cultural construction of the visual in arts, media, and everyday life' (Dikovitskaya 2005: 1). As such it has a literature of its own, and its detailed exploration goes beyond the scope of the present survey (as it is the case for *cultural studies*, of which the visual are partly a by-product). Some references are given in the following section, Suggestions for further reading. What is important to register here is the significance of the new horizons for interpretation of the past that this perspective is opening up. On one hand, we have acquired new awareness of the historical diversity of the iconic forms of representation of reality. Via a variety of approaches, however, scholars in the field are exposing changes not simply in the way the world has been represented, but also in the way it has been perceived. As the media revolution of the mid-twentieth century triggered the historical inventiveness of McLuhan and others, it may be precisely because we live at the time of the triumph of vision that we have become more aware of its historical conditions.[17] The American art historian Jonathan Crary (1990) – who dates to the early nineteenth century a rupture with the Renaissance, or *classical*, modes of seeing, and the origins of visual modernity, and finds his evidence in the diffusion of new optical devices and in a renewed intellectual interest in the observer as subject of philosophical and scientific discourse – identifies the development of our time that has made us aware of previous sensory revolutions in the 'dematerialized digital image'. In whatever way we define it, it would be difficult to deny that our visual experience is undergoing dramatic and prolonged processes of change.

Epilogue

In light of the above-mentioned characteristics of a cultural history of media, it is possible to specify what distinguishes this orientation in modern research and, for instance, differentiates it from the perspective we continue to call intellectual history (see Chapter 3). The former is normally characterized by the recourse to a variety of authors and texts, including humble ones, for this reason representative of an average discourse (rather than emphasizing the role of protagonists and key witnesses). Furthermore, it implies attention to the forms of cultural reception, rather than exclusively to those of production.

The distinction between the two interpretive modes can be approached effectively by giving the example of the contribution that Chartier (1991), a leading representative of the new style, has made to an old historiographical question – the search for the roots of the French Revolution. Departing from the old thesis of its *intellectual* origins (the historical changes seen as the result of the circulation of a given number of ideas, to sum up the product of the circle of Enlightenment philosophers), he has proposed to substitute it with that of *cultural* roots: exposure of a previously inexperienced French public to a variety and quantity of forms and practices of reading (gazettes, pamphlets and novels, as well as – or else, rather than – treatises) that created a new sensitivity and openness to change. When the course of events confronted men and women with decisions they were largely responsible for making, a wide mental orientation to what is new would emerge, one that would not have been conceivable without the eighteenth-century adventures of reading.

The American historian William Bouwsma clearly expressed his preference for the expression *cultural history* rather than *intellectual history* in the opening pages of his last important book:

> The explanation for this substitution is that the term 'intellectual' is not historically neutral. Indeed, it begs a large question basic to studies of this kind, for it presupposes the existence of a faculty, perhaps an organ vaguely identified with the brain, that is itself a 'high' thing, as the head is considered, by some obscure design implicit in our creation or biology, the highest part of the body. This organ, the *intellect*, is sometimes thought to make possible human concern with 'higher things'. But this notion is itself, of course, no more than a cultural artefact, a legacy from the Greeks to which we subliminally cling, even if it is singularly discordant with the otherwise dominant culture of the modern world. It is also, as a label, unduly restrictive, since it suggests a particular value attaching to abstract thought, to 'ideas', to the productions of those human beings whom we describe as "intellectuals', a group with which historians have usually had little difficulty in identifying themselves. Only recently have they displayed much interest in the presumably 'lower' aspects of the self, as in the – not unrelated – 'lower' levels of society.
>
> (Bouwsma 2000: IX)

What is curious is that the author of these remarks had been for his whole career a rather traditional type of intellectual historian; and that the quoted passage introduces the late-Renaissance volume in a series entitled 'Yale *Intellectual* History'.[18] One is inclined to infer that, while distinctions between different approaches may be useful, they do not erect impermeable barriers between them. Further recent signs seem to point in the same direction.[19]

Current research points in a variety of different directions, and it would not be a particularly easy or helpful exercise here to try to guess the leading paths of the near future. A few strings, however, may be tied together from orientations we encountered throughout this short book. In an age aware and concerned with trends of globalization, and with cultural exchange and questions of hybrid identity at the forefront of public discourse (see Chapter 3), world or global history is likely to feature prominently in patterns of research and education. A book such as Fernández-Armesto's *Pathfinders* (2006), with the human drive to exploration as its topic, and the globe and human history over the past million-and-a-half years as its territory, can suggest at least one line of enquiry we are likely to see followed. Delving deep into the past of humankind has been recommended in the form of a deep history that deals seriously with the time before civilization, thus fully considering the Palaeolithic era and dropping the separate status of prehistory; by looking into the genetic and archaeological archives, a first sketch of this story has been put forward as one that can account for long-term developments in human behaviour (Smail 2008).[20] As we have hinted when touching on the possibility of a psychohistory (Chapter 1), or the recent boom in studies of the emotions (Chapter 4), here history meets biology and the question of evolution. Within a neo-Darwinian agenda, another wide-ranging theoretical contribution has now proposed the distinction between a natural, a cultural and a social selection, each influencing individual human behaviour by a mode of its own – evocation, acquisition and imposition, respectively (Runciman 2009). To what extent trends like these will be compatible with a culturalist approach that has put emphasis on human agency and symbolic language, or whether they will command some other paradigm shift, remains to be seen.

Summary

A culturalist perspective can significantly enrich a wide variety of areas of enquiry. Social hierarchy itself – the central research object of social history – incorporates important cultural aspects, such as identities and representations of the world. The more recent addition of gender history also provides a major incentive to study cultural factors: one just needs to think of social roles and value systems. Rather than focusing exclusively on individuals or groups, cultural history shows the potential of studying the intersection between the two spheres.

The history of the body is a frontier of current research that represents well the novelty of the culturalist approach. It comprises specific components – such as the history of health and disease, or that of systems of punishment and modes of confinement – but has emerged as something more than their sum. It shows how the cultural viewpoint allows the incorporation of topics that past historiographies would have assigned to the worlds of nature, or else of nearly static social structures. As an effect, this new agenda and its findings have changed the shape of history as a whole.

If we consider the whole range of phenomena that are studied by cultural historians, the history of the media – and of the book and reading in particular – appears as a privileged field of enquiry. As well as registering change in the historical forms of cultural supply, the most innovative and inspired scholarship has valued the importance of consumption: the uses (including the unforeseen) and appropriations that characterize the actual circulation of texts and artefacts and contribute, no less than authors or contexts of production, to determining its effects.

Notes

1 The expression was introduced in 1967 by Guy Debord (1994), and belongs to a series of tools for a critical interpretation of contemporary society that has a parallel, for instance, in the 'consumer society' (Baudrillard 1998, 2005) and has produced the tradition of politically engaged social studies also characteristic of *cultural studies*, from their cradle in the Birmingham Centre for Contemporary Cultural Studies (1964–). Influential among the political movements of the late 1960s, Debord's theses were a Marxist critique of commodity fetishism, centred on a negative judgment of the influence mass media had on people.

2 An expression used, for instance, by Mitchell (2005b).

3 With deliberate simplification, it has been suggested that 'nineteenth-century European nations with colonies tended to develop an anthropological study of primitive societies, while the ethnographic interest in countries with few or no colonies was first directed to the "primitive within", the rapidly disintegrating peasant culture' (Frykman and Löfgren 1987: 2). The project of which the quoted book is part was started at the Department of European Ethnology of the University of Lund.

4 In the French scholar's definition, 'a *lieu de mémoire* is any significant entity, whether material or non-material in nature, which by dint of human will or the work of time has become a symbolic element of the memorial heritage of any community' (Nora 1996–98, Vol. I: vii; see also Green 2008: 101–3). The project also inspired applications to Dutch, German, Italian, North American and Spanish history.

5 On the historical construction of the category of youth in France, see Cohen (2010).

6 Not far from Ariès is the orientation expressed by Badinter (1981) for the specific history of maternal love.

7 Citation from the otherwise not unsympathetic review by Denise Riley, *History Workshop*, 29 (1990): 147–50.

8 The related notion of 'haptic' refers to a combined visual and tactile experience (Paterson 2007).

9 A similar process of cultural construction of collective memory has suggested seeing 'imagined communities' as the root of nationalism (Anderson 1991).

10 Carnival was also the subject of a major research in the Iberian traditions by historical ethnographer Julio Caro Baroja (1965), a scholar also responsible for an investigation in the field of witchcraft (Caro Baroja 1964).

11 Raffaella Sarti (2004) is an Italian scholar who has worked on similar lines on a European scale, by revisiting forms and tools of dwelling, eating and dressing in the early modern period.

12 The continuing importance of a manuscript tradition and the way it combined with print is the focus of a Spanish school of cultural history, which has explored in detail the early modern experience at the heart of the country's literary heritage and at the height of its imperial power (Bouza 2001; Castillo Gómez 2006).

13 A dialogue among the two French scholars can be read in Reeser and Spaldin (2002).

14 On the origins of the latter, see Saenger (1997).

15 In different ways, in the late 1960s French theorists Roland Barthes (1915–80) and Michel Foucault influentially commented on the author function or registered a 'death of the author' (Barthes 1977; Foucault 1977b). Foucault also made a similar point in his inaugural lecture at the Collège de France (Foucault 1973).

16 A Dutch-centred Centre for the Study of Egodocuments and History (with links to egodocuments in the European context) has its web site at www. egodocument.net/egodocument/index.html. Influential theoretical reflections on autobiographical writing (with historical implications, up to online diaries and the blogosphere) have been proposed by French critic Philippe Lejeune; Sidonie Smith and Julia Watson have reflected on autobiography and gender.

17 Having said that, the reader should be reminded that, as we have mentioned above, the story of the supposed primacy of one or another sense has been narrated in sharply different ways, and the cultural importance of sight has not been safe from negative prejudice and evaluation: Martin Jay (1993) explores this side of twentieth-century French thought. The very notion of the predominance of one sense, and particularly the isolation of the visual from the remaining ones, as if they worked in isolation, is contested by Mitchell (2005a), who concludes: 'It is because there are no visual media that we need a concept of visual culture'.

18 Bouwsma's choice is discussed by Brett (2002).

19 A confirmation of such a deduction seems to come from the subject and the tone of some of the texts that have been written to celebrate the career of the cultural historian Peter Burke. This was hinted, for instance, in the introduction by the editors of a volume dedicated to Burke on his retirement: intellectual history may usually be understood as serious and precise study of systems of thought, while cultural history is seen as vaguer but more imaginative; however, they share an interest in theory, and a focus on a broad range of texts and their contexts (Calaresu *et al.* 2010: 7–10). In the above-mentioned passage, Joan Pau Rubiés speaks of a *missed* encounter between disciplines; nevertheless, his comments suggest that increasing interaction between the two fields should be expected. Questions concerning the precision of the discipline and its relationship with theory were also

raised by Peter Mandler (2004) and by other contributors to the forum subsequently opened by the journal *Cultural and Social History*. On another such occasion, a seminar on 'polyphonic history' held in Madrid in 2008, Burke himself suggested, of intellectual and cultural history: 'The frontier between the two is increasingly transgressed, producing a hybrid that we might describe as the cultural history of ideas, or better, perhaps, the cultural history of intellectual practices' (Burke 2010b: 482).

20 Barnard (2011) makes the point that human origins can be studied by social anthropology, and should not be seen as the preserve of biological or physical anthropology.

Suggestions for further reading

Peter Burke is author of the most successful (and widely translated) among the available guides to this field (Burke 2008b). His book is organized chronologically, and offers a personal panorama of generations and orientations in cultural history, from the 'great tradition' of Burckhardt and Huizinga to the present scene, and the one foreseeable or desirable for the near future. This approach is made particularly interesting by the fact that it comes from one of the protagonists of the genre: an author known for his curiosity in exploring different paths of research, and who therefore can directly give personal examples – as well as those by colleagues – of the varying paradigms that have oriented cultural history writing over the past few decades. The different arrangement presented by my book should hopefully make the two mutually compatible and to some extent complementary. A further point should be made about Burke's organization of material. This is not a pure choice in presentation: Burke denies that a definite common denominator can be found among all the different ways of doing cultural history; consequently, because of the discipline's loose definition and intrinsic polyphony, the only descriptive option left is to explore its historical varieties. Or, to put it in Ludmilla Jordanova's words (2006: 14): 'History, the discipline, is indeed about what historians do'.

Among the recent additions to the family of short introductions, Anna Green's (2008) volume – which appeared within a particularly helpful Palgrave series on 'Theory and History', directed by Donald MacRaild – is more theoretically oriented than others. Coming from an Australian scholar whose main area of expertise is oral history, it gives particular emphasis to issues of remembering and collective memory.

Since the year 2000, an increasing number of introductions to cultural history have also been published in other languages. In French, the modernist Pascal Ory (2004) wrote the cultural history title within the popular pocket-book series 'Que sais-je?' (a series within which the reader of French will find interesting items also on the *imaginaire*, symbol and many other related subjects). Ory's volume aims more systematically than others at theoretically defining the field and distinguishing it from neighbouring ones. Another modernist, Philippe Poirrier, is the author of a more detailed and bibliographically exact examination, in this case specifically devoted to the French historiographical experience, from the generation of the history of mentalities until current trends, including such specialities as the history of intellectuals (Poirrier 2004). Poirrier is also the editor of a collective volume in which an international team of scholars draws a portrait of the field as it has developed in various countries (Poirrier 2008).[1]

A volume with a similar agenda is being edited in English by Jörg Rogge, the result of a conference on 'Cultural History in Europe: institutions – themes – perspectives', held in Mainz in 2010. In German, Ute Daniel (2001) has provided a successful compendium, reprinted several times to serve the growing academic market in our field in that linguistic domain. Her introduction is also one of the most substantial in size, thus allowing for a reasonable selection of trends and topics of research, and of keywords. Like others, she starts from the final decades of the nineteenth century. However, her main interest in that period is not so much a search for precedents to more recent historiography: it is, rather, an empathy with the epistemological debates by which, at the turn of the century, the academic status of humanities as a field of knowledge was assessed and contrasted with natural sciences. Daniel believes those reflections are still highly relevant to our work today.

After Daniel, a series of other German publications went through the press, which bear to varying degrees the character of textbooks for study at university level (Germany is today, arguably, the most significant country where a prospective student can major in cultural history from the undergraduate stage all the way through a dedicated doctoral course). Maurer (2008) has offered a systematic and original examination of fifteen topics, including the culture of names (of people or places), the culture of languages and the languages of culture (the subsequent international role of Latin, French and English as forms of communication), the culture of tradition (cultural and educational institutions) and of time and space. Tschopp and Weber (2006) surveyed controversies in cultural history, and discussed texts, images and symbolic acts as the most representative types of source. Tschopp (2008) has collected an anthology of key statements of the principles and methods of the discipline, from Burckhardt to the present.

Landwehr and Stockhorst (2004) have produced an updated teaching aid, introducing students to the cultural history of Europe.[2]

In Danish, Christiansen (2000) wrote a history of cultural history from nineteenth-century Germany, focusing on Denmark and on Troels Frederik Troels-Lund (1840–1921), a historian who undertook a vast reconstruction of the material culture and daily life of the Scandinavian people in the sixteenth century, in significant synchronicity with the development of the study of folklore. Both in this specific case and in his following depiction of twentieth-century historiography, Christiansen's main point is that cultural history is a kind of historiographical counterculture, with a vocation for opposing the establishment that is dominant at any time.[3]

Readers of Spanish may find useful both a translation of Daniel's volume[4] and a book by Serna and Pons (2005). The latter takes the form of a guided tour of the internationally most representative centres of cultural history, suggesting that the development of the discipline has been primarily the work of an 'invisible college', a network of first-rank specialists – featuring Burke, Chartier, Darnton, Davis and Ginzburg – whose research is closely related and mutually referential.[5] The definition of the field is also attracting interest in Latin America, as the published proceedings of a seminar held by Colombian and Mexican historians and sociologists testifies (Rodríguez Gonzáles 2004). In Portuguese, in a short essay, Falcon (2002) assigns cultural history a place within the problematic panorama of contemporary historiography, by discussing such issues as the name of the field (cultural history or history of culture?). Textbooks are now appearing in a variety of languages including, for instance, Romanian (Lung 2009 – on both worldwide paradigms and the national tradition).

The reader of Italian – the original language of the present book – has currently, among others, the opportunity for a preview of the vision a leading American cultural historian, Lynn Hunt, has of the discipline 'in the global era' (Hunt 2010 – at the time of writing, a text not planned to appear in English). In it, she considers the rise of cultural history and the problems posed by its lack of paradigms; defines globalization and discusses the challenges it poses to historians; affirms the need to learn from the approaches of non-Western historians, rethinking the role of historical causation, and paying new attention to the influence of the individual self in history; and, finally, postulates the want of a new metanarrative (or high historical generalization), one that may grow out of the pros and cons of its precedents, from Hegel to Foucault.

Back in the English-language world, a variety of sub-genres and individual volumes are relevant to the present area of study and can offer plenty of opportunities for in-depth analysis or the widening of horizons: I can mention only a few here. Gunn (2006) has offered a thought-provoking survey of the relevance of cultural theory to history (somehow at a border line between cultural history and cultural studies): it covers such issues as power, modernity and identity. Clark (2004) has produced an interesting volume with a fairly similar agenda, focusing on the linguistic turn and specifically addressing scholars of the early Christian literature, in order to show them what they could gain by taking theory into due consideration. Jordanova (2006) has provided readers with an acclaimed guide to history, which does not have a particular field as its object, but gives a view of the discipline – its status and trends – from the perspective of a practising cultural historian. Naturally, sections on cultural history can be found within books of wider scope, or in books on neighbouring or overlapping fields of specialization. This is particularly true for the case of social history, which, as I have aimed to show in Chapter 1, is the most closely related. So it is not a surprise if a book on the latter and its relation with social theory ends with a chapter entitled 'Ideology, *mentalité* and social ritual: from social history to cultural history' (MacRaild and Taylor 2004: 118–51). The reader can find similar interest in the literature on intellectual history (Whatmore and Young 2006). As for religious history, which also underwent many developments connected with our topic, a synthetic sketch with suggestions for further reading, which includes reference to the linguistic turn and identity formation, is offered by Hufton (2002).

Further, specific reading opportunities are available on the whole range of research topics and orientations covered in this book. For instance, visual studies (see Chapter 4) is a comparatively young field that in a short time has developed a significant bibliography, inclusive of specialized journals. Given the fact that it has hardly reached any form of consensus on its very definition of object, scope and method (Mitchell 2002), it is best approached via a series of introductions and readers (Bryson *et al.* 1994; Jenks 1995; Walker and Chaplin 1997; Evans and Hall 1999; Howells 2003; Mirzoeff 2006; Morra and Smith 2006), some of which include interviews with protagonists in the field (Dikovitskaya 2005; Smith 2008).

As we have already hinted, *cultural studies* also have a conspicuous literature of their own, which includes many introductions and readers. It may be worth registering that the latter have now appeared in languages other than English – though, as a reminiscence of their place of origin, they have retained the English denomination of the field (see Lutter and Reisenleitner 1998, available in both German and Italian).

The same may be said for related areas such as communication, media and film studies.

Notes

1 The Italian version (a Spanish one is also on its way) presents a slightly different selection of countries.
2 There is no room here for detailed reference to cultural histories of Europe in general, or of any other specific area or period, for that matter. The sketch of the nineteenth century offered by Hannu Salmi (2008), however, deserves mention, at least as a document of cultural history as it is currently practised in northern European countries.
3 For a (linguistically) more widely accessible synthesis on cultural history in Scandinavia also featuring Troels-Lund, see Christiansen's contribution to Poirrier's collection (Christiansen 2008). On Troels-Lund, see Burke (2004a).
4 *Compendio de historia cultural*, Madrid: Alianza, 2005.
5 The same two scholars had previously authored a volume (Serna and Pons 2000) characterized by the slightly unusual agenda of describing and discussing the work of a single cultural historian, the Italian Carlo Ginzburg, and focusing predominantly on one of his books, *The Cheese and the Worms* (Ginzburg 1980).

Appendix
Selected cultural historians and influential cultural theorists – some short biographies[1]

Philippe Ariès

Philippe Ariès (1914–84) was one of the protagonists of the French tradition of research in the history of mentalities (see Chapter 3). While he originally was no professional historian, he concluded his career as director of studies at the École des Hautes Études en Sciences Sociales (EHESS), Paris. His most representative contributions were an influential, though contested, reconstruction of the history of childhood (Ariès 1996; see Chapter 4), and a study of historical attitudes towards death (*L'Homme devant la mort*, 1977), both chronologically wide-ranging. He was also actively involved in collective works on various aspects of daily life (see for instance Ariès and Duby 1987–91), including play in the Renaissance (Daileader and Whalen 2010: 11–22).

Mikhail Bakhtin

Mikhail Bakhtin (1895–1975) was a Russian literary critic with interests and influences across many disciplines. His posthumous fortune predominantly rests on *Rabelais and His World* (Bakhtin 1984, a dissertation first published in Russian in 1965, and for which he had originally been denied the doctorate), a study of the French Renaissance literary master in the context of the popular culture of 'carnivalesque' (play, laughter and the world upside down); and on *The Dialogic Imagination* (1975), a series of essays that popularized such notions as 'dialogism' (which emphasizes the relational nature of everything that is said, always a response to something else) or 'heteroglossia' (the idea that every linguistic code is hybrid, polyphonic and internally conflicting).

Michael Baxandall

Michael Baxandall (1933–2008) has been an inspirational art critic for both his original research and his theoretical reflections. Among other institutions, he held posts at the Warburg Institute, London and at the University of California, Berkeley. He introduced the notion of 'period eye', suggesting that viewers belonging to a given culture shared a vocabulary and perspective that later could not be taken for granted and may need recovering – arguably the most characteristic and fruitful assumption for any *cultural* history of art to make sense (see Chapter 4). He paid attention to the practical aspects of the production of art as well as the available documents of a period, and was interested in theories of perception (see www.dictionaryofarthistorians.org).

Marc Bloch

Marc Bloch (1886–1944) was a specialist in the history of serfdom, feudalism and French rural history; his research also aimed at reconstructing 'modes of feeling and thought', and included, for instance, a depiction of medieval perceptions of time. He had a vivid interest in collective consciousness (a domain in which he was influenced by the sociology of Émile Durkheim), which he expressed in a study of the circulation of rumours (during World War I) and in his fundamental *The Royal Touch* (Bloch 1973, originally published in 1924; see Chapter 3). (On his friendship with Lucien Febvre and the co-foundation of the *Annales*, see Febvre's entry within this Appendix.) Bloch fought in the Resistance against the Nazi occupation of France and was executed by German troops after his capture. He was an advocate of the use of comparison in history, and left unfinished wellknown methodological reflections, which were published posthumously by Febvre (*The Historian's Craft*, 1949) (Burke 1990: 12–27; Hughes-Warrington 2008: 11–19; Daileader and Whalen 2010: 38–61).

Pierre Bourdieu

Pierre Bourdieu (1920–2002) taught at the EHESS and at the École Normale Supérieure, Paris; from 1982 he also held the chair of sociology at the Collège de France. He combined insightful theory with empirical research, and produced an original sociology of culture, which was based on a broad notion of capital (social, cultural and symbolic); explained the dynamics of social distinction (his *Distinction*, 1982 is regarded as one of the most important works in twentieth-century sociology); and analysed the embodiment of structures of action (habitus).

Fernand Braudel

Fernand Braudel (1902–85) succeeded Lucien Febvre both at the Collège de France and as editor of the *Annales*. Also an early modernist, he wrote *The Mediterranean and the Mediterranean World in the Age of Philip II* (1949) while in captivity in German prisoner camps during World War II. It includes a highly influential presentation of a three-tiered historical time: the deep and slow-moving ecological structures; the slightly faster time of social trends; and the superficial, individual time of events. This gaze can be seen as an original re-elaboration of the Marxist relationship between structure and superstructure, and in this way provided an authoritative assessment of the relation between culture and society. His further work on capitalism has inspired the interpretation of the economy as a world system. Although he could be regarded as the French historian who most oriented decades of research towards socio-economic factors and collective structures, rather than culture and individual agency, his notion of *civilisation materielle* (material culture) was rich in reference to fashions and customs (see Chapter 1; Burke 1990: 32–64; Hughes-Warrington 2008: 20–28; Daileader and Whalen 2010: 62–76).

John Brewer

Currently Professor at the California Institute of Technology, John Brewer (1947–) was educated at Cambridge and has taught at several American universities, as well as working as a consultant to museums and galleries. He studied the politics and culture of eighteenth-century Britain and co-edited seminal work on the early modern culture of consumption. More recently, he has reflected upon microhistory as a form of historical practice and has written one example of his own (*A Sentimental Murder*, 2004). He is also studying the world of art collecting, in collaboration with the Getty Museum (Snowman 2007: 244–55).

Peter Brown

Born in Ireland, Peter Brown (1935–) has taught in Oxford (where he had studied), London, Berkeley and Princeton. He is regarded as the creator of late antiquity as a field of study in its own right (rather than simply as the end of the Roman world). He has explored early Christianity – in particular, since his book on Augustine of Hippo (1967), the role of saints – in terms of a historical anthropology of religious belief and practice; his research topics include Roman rhetoric, the body and sexuality, and wealth and poverty.

Jacob Burckhardt

Jacob Burckhardt (1818–97) studied history at the University of Berlin, where he attended lectures by Leopold von Ranke. However, he subsequently returned to teach in his native Basel, and turned down offers for prestigious academic positions in Germany. His writing rested on a philosophy of history that regarded the state, religion and culture as three powers, whose interaction determined the course of human events (Burckhardt 1943). He was a pioneer of a total history encompassing all aspects of a period, as the table of contents of his hugely influential portrait of the Italian Renaissance (Burckhardt 1990) shows: The State as a Work of Art; The Development of the Individual; The Revival of Antiquity; The Discovery of the World and of Man; Society and Festivals; Morality and Religion. He was a passionate expert of Italian art, for which he wrote a reference travel guide (*Cicerone*, 1855) (see Chapter 2; White 1973: 230–64; Hinde 2000; Daniel 2001: 200–207; Sigurdson 2004).

Peter Burke

Peter Burke (1937–) taught Early Modern European and Cultural History at the universities of Sussex and Cambridge. He displayed an interest in the relationship between the practice of history and the social sciences (*History and Social Theory*, 1992), and applied it first to the Italian Renaissance by setting art and literature in the context of contemporary society. In *Popular Culture in Early Modern Europe* (1978), he offered a classic study of the interaction between the cultures of different social groups. He is sensitive to the social uses of knowledge (*A Social History of Knowledge*, 2000; *A Social History of the Media*, with Asa Briggs, 2002) and aware of the linguistic variable (*Languages and Communities in Early Modern Europe*, 2004). He has also shown a curiosity about intercultural comparison, and reflected on the history and perspectives of cultural encounters (*Cultural Hybridity*, 2009). (On Burke 2008b, see Suggestions for further reading.) (Pallares-Burke 2002: 129–57; Snowman 2007: 41–49; Calaresu *et al.* 2010: 1–28; del Río Barredo 2010).

Caroline Walker Bynum

Caroline Walker Bynum (1941–), an expert in the religious ideas and practices of the European Middle Ages, has taught at Harvard, the University of Washington, Columbia and the Institute of Advanced Study, Princeton. She has pioneered the perspective of gender in medieval studies (Bynum 1987) and offered remarkable examples of a history of the body (*Fragmentation and Redemption*, 1991; *The Resurrection of the Body in Western Christianity*, 1995). She has studied blood piety in northern Germany (*Wonderful Blood*, 2007), the role of objects in late medieval religion and devotional practices in an inter-religious comparative perspective.

Michel de Certeau

Michel de Certeau (1925–86), a Jesuit, was an intellectual and polymath interested in a multiplicity of fields of knowledge, including the philosophy of history, psychoanalysis, ethnology and the study of religions, as well as cultural history. He held university posts in Paris and San Diego. In his capacity as historian of spirituality, he studied in particular seventeenth-century mysticism. However, he is more widely known for his reflections on the writing of history; for the topic of otherness, explored in a variety of sources including ethnography in the age of European expansion; and, above all, for his observations on the practice of everyday life and the independent agency played by individuals (Certeau 1984; Frijhoff 2010; see also Chapter 4).

Roger Chartier

Roger Chartier (1945–) was director of studies at the EHESS and has subsequently been elected to a chair at the Collège de France (on writing and cultures in early modern Europe). He is one of the best-known French historians, with an international reputation and network particularly significant in the Iberian peninsula and in the Americas. From the early stages of his career, he engaged in questions of method and historiography. He has practically reinvented the field of the history of the book (see Chapter 4) by broadening its scope and livening it up, with emphasis on the practices of reading and the variety of uses of texts (Serna and Pons 2005: 100–114, 155–72; Daileader and Whalen 2010: 93–104).

Stuart Clark

Stuart Clark taught early modern history at the University of Wales, Swansea. His approach to the history of witchcraft (see Chapter 3) has been unique in the extent to which it framed belief in the supernatural within the contemporary 'ordinary' mind. The role that vision played in that story led him to investigate further the status of sight in the Western system of senses. The result (see Chapter 4) is a much more nuanced and troubled account than McLuhan's narrative of the triumph of the eye over the ear. Although it could be difficult to choose whether to assign Clark to cultural or intellectual history, that only proves the limits of pigeon holes.

Linda Colley

Linda Colley (1949–), a specialist of eighteenth-century British and imperial history, has taught at Yale and Princeton universities, among other institutions. She has studied the development of a sense of British national identity (*Britons*, 1992) and the narratives and diverse destinies of the British men, women and children who were captured, whether in the Mediterranean, in Asia or in North America (*Captives*, 2002). Her interest in the connection between individual biographies and global developments is further testified by her story of the life of a woman who travelled the world further than any other had done (Colley 2007). She is married to the historian David Cannadine (Snowman 2007: 187–97).

Alain Corbin

A specialist in the nineteenth century, Alain Corbin (1936–) is a versatile French social and cultural historian who has studied topics as diverse as prostitution and related practices and tastes (*Women for Hire*, 1978); changing attitudes toward the sea and coasts (*The Lure of the Sea*, 1988); a case of rage and murder (*The Village of Cannibals*, 1990); and a randomly chosen member of a community (*The Life of an Unknown*, 1998), as well as festivals, leisure and the barricade. He is particularly known for his exploration of emotions and the sensory, with studies of odours (Corbin 1986, 1995; see Chapter 4) and of the 'auditory landscape' of the countryside (*Village Bells*, 1994) (Daileader and Whalen 2010: 136–43).

Robert Darnton

Professor of history at Princeton for forty years, Robert Darnton (1939–), now University Professor and Director of the Harvard University Library, is a distinguished scholar of eighteenth-century France, with a special expertise in the history of the book. In particular, he has examined practices of publishing (including the publishing history of Diderot and d'Alembert's *Encyclopédie*) and of reading. His interest is not limited to the masterpieces of the Enlightenment, however, and characteristically includes the pornographic literature of the time, 'forbidden best-sellers'. He has attracted attention to the role played by Parisian coffee houses in the circulation of information and thoughts (Darnton 2000; see Chapter 3), as well as by poems and songs (*Poetry and the Police*, 2010). He has also participated in methodological discussions on history, and offered a classic example of historical anthropology (Darnton 1984; see Chapter 1; Pallares-Burke 2002: 158–83; Serna and Pons 2005: 145–54).

Lorraine Daston

The American scholar Lorraine Daston (1951–) is Director of the Max Planck Institute for the History of Science in Berlin, is Visiting Professor in the Committee on Social Thought at the University of Chicago, and has taught in several other institutions worldwide. Her topics of research include the classical theory of probability, the emergence of the scientific fact, scientific models, 'things that talk' (see Chapter 4), the moral authority of nature, monsters and marvels (*Wonders and the Order of Nature*, 2001, with Katharine Park), as well as scientific images and notions of truth-to-nature (*Objectivity*, 2007, with Peter Galison).

Natalie Zemon Davis

Professor Emerita at the University of Toronto, where in the early 1970s she taught one of the earliest courses in women's history, Natalie Zemon Davis (1928–), who also taught at Berkeley and Princeton, is one of the most authoritative members of the historical profession worldwide. A scholar of sixteenth-century France, she has pioneered historical anthropology by providing models of study of ritual practice, from the gift to urban violence. The case of mistaken identity that made her name popular among a wide readership (Davis 1983; see Chapter 1) is characteristic of a range of historical questions to which she has subsequently paid continuous attention: in more recent research she explored the relation between personal and religious identity in a series of individuals somehow belonging to more than one world (Davis 1995, 2006). She also reflected on the relation between film and historical vision in the case of the representation of slavery

(*Slaves on Screen*, 2000) (Pallares-Burke 2002: 50–79; Serna and Pons 2005: 49–66, 130–37; Snowman 2007: 175–86; Hughes-Warrington 2008: 53–60).

Georges Duby

French medievalist Georges Duby (1919–96) taught at Aix-en-Provence and at the Collège de France. After working on the rural economy and feudal society, as well as on kinship, marriage and lineage, he came to affirm 'the centrality of beliefs, attitudes and memories in determining human actions, and thereafter became preoccupied with recovering the realm of "the medieval imagery"' (Evergates 1997: 651). Religious art, chronicle accounts of the Battle of Bouvines (1214), chivalry, the lives of twelfth-century women and the imagined tri-partition of society provided some of the terrain for such an enquiry. He co-edited major collective works on the history of private life and on the history of women in the West. His narrative style was powerful; however, his work proved methodologically unconvincing for part of the scholarly community (Daileader and Whalen 2010: 180–201).

Elizabeth L. Eisenstein

Elizabeth Lewisohn Eisenstein (1923–) is Professor Emerita of history at the University of Michigan. She has produced a reference assessment of the impact of the printing press, which in her opinion has produced a medium with distinctive features and noticeable effects on the Renaissance, the Reformation and the Scientific Revolution (Eisenstein 1979, 1993 – the latter including the author's reply to her critics). She also studied the partial dependence of eighteenth-century French readers on imported books and journals (*Grub Street Abroad*, 1992). Her *Divine Art, Infernal Machine* (2010) is an account of five centuries of ambivalent attitudes toward printing and printers.

Norbert Elias

Norbert Elias (1897–1990), a German Jew who spent a large part of his career in Britain and Amsterdam, was one of the sociologists who most influenced twentieth-century historical research. His work centred on the idea of a civilizing process, which he studied in the form of the diffusion of increasingly demanding social etiquette (Elias 1994), as well as the regulated life of court society (Elias 2006). His metanarrative has been challenged as ethnocentric, as it seems to imply that men and women from different epochs and cultures were incapable of the self-control that would appear to be characteristic of the modern West. He also studied the historical taming of sports violence (Elias and Dunning 1986; see Chapter 4; for a series of reviews of his work see Chartier 1997: 105–43).

Arlette Farge

Arlette Farge is *directrice de recherche* at the Centre National de la Recherche Scientifique in Paris. She is a historian of the eighteenth century interested in the behaviour of ordinary people – the crowd, public opinion (*Subversive Words*, 1992), the body and sensitivities – as well as in the writing of history and the relations between men and women. The material for her books comes from judicial archives: 'the odd scrap, snatch of a phrase, fragments of lives from that vast repository of once-pronounced words that constitute the archives' (Farge 1993:1); recovering the voices of people from the past has been her specific aspiration.

Lucien Febvre

Lucien Febvre (1878–1956) was the promoter of a broad notion of history, not limited to politics and warfare but informed by a wide range of social sciences. In *A Geographical Introduction to History* (1922) he emphasized the different responses human beings give to the environment, and the role played by society. Before taking up a chair at the Collège de France in Paris, he taught at Strasbourg, where he developed collaboration with the medievalist Marc Bloch. Together, they founded *Annales*, the influential journal that would disseminate their approach to history internationally. One of his main areas of research was religious belief and the choices available to men and women of the past (Febvre 1982, originally published in 1942; see Chapter 3; Burke 1990: 12–33; Hughes-Warrington 2008: 100–107).

Felipe Fernández-Armesto

Felipe Fernández-Armesto (1950–), a historian frequently present in the media, has taught both in Great Britain (Oxford, Queen Mary) and the USA (Tufts, Notre Dame). From an expertise in the history of exploration (Fernández-Armesto 2006, plus books on Columbus and Vespucci), he has developed an appetite for the challenge of wide geographical and chronological perspectives (*Millennium*, 1995;

Ideas, 2003), with particular interest in the way human groups have faced different environments (*Civilizations*, 2000). Topics of specific enquiry in some of his books are food, truth and the concept of humankind.

Paula Findlen

Professor of Italian history and chair of the Department of history at Stanford University, Paula Findlen is a specialist in Renaissance scientific knowledge that has emphasized its connection with humanistic approaches to the world (in an age in which it had not yet developed its current autonomy as a field); is interested in the relations between gender, culture and knowledge; and has studied the practices of collecting (*Possessing Nature*, 1994), often in collaboration with other scholars.

Michel Foucault

Michel Foucault (1926–84) is a distinctively unlikely candidate for a Twitter-length biography. Although his background essentially qualifies him as a philosopher, he developed a distinguished interest in historical analysis, and opened up entire digging sites for future research (the archaeological metaphor was one of his favourite). Diverse as his topics have been, they expressed a common, continuous preoccupation with a critique of the Western notion of 'subject', that is, an exaggerated emphasis on the individual, whom he saw rather as the product of historical techniques, combining power and knowledge (on his courses at the Collège de France and much else, see Chapters 3 and 4; O'Brien 1989; Daniel 2001: 167–78; Hughes-Warrington 2008: 107–16; Daileader and Whalen 2010: 252–70).

Willem Frijhoff

W. T. M. Frijhoff (1942–) is Professor of early modern history at the VU-University, Amsterdam and a prominent Dutch cultural historian. In the 1970s he was research assistant at the Centre for European religious anthropology at the EHESS in Paris and studied, with Dominique Julia, the French school system of the Ancien Régime. As well as the history of early modern education, his research interests include the religious history of Europe and North America, from interconfessional holiness to the survival strategies of minority groups (Roodenburg 2010).

Peter Gay

Born in Berlin (as Peter Frölich), but educated in the USA after his family fled Nazi Germany, Peter Gay (1923–) taught history and political science at Columbia and Yale universities. Among many other subjects, he has published books on the cultural history of the Enlightenment and of the Weimar Republic, on Mozart, Arthur Schnitzler and modernism in the arts. However, his name is particularly associated with a prolonged interest in the social impact of psychoanalysis and an exploration of its potential use for history (Gay 1985).

Clifford Geertz

The work of Clifford James Geertz (1926–2006), and particularly his essay on the Balinese cockfight, has become the obsessively standard reference for historians interested in experimenting with anthropological tools (to the extent that – as it is now often lamented – few historians are properly informed of the much wider and diverse methodological offer which is available on the anthropological market, so to speak). He taught anthropology and social sciences at the University of Chicago and the Institute for Advanced Study, Princeton. His exploration of the meaning of culture emphasized the importance of shared symbolism and incorporated an appreciation of *Local Knowledge* (the title of his second collection of essays, 1983; on his notion of culture and model of 'thick description', see Chapter 1; Serna and Pons 2005: 138–44).

Carlo Ginzburg

Carlo Ginzburg (1939–) is arguably the Italian historian with whose name an international audience is most familiar. He has taught at the University of Bologna, at the University of California, Los Angeles (UCLA) and at the Scuola Normale Superiore, Pisa. As an early modernist he has notably worked with influential books on Inquisition trials (Ginzburg 1980, 1983). While his original discovery of the interaction between the Inquisition and the *benandanti* of north-east Italy could be understood as an evidence of witchcraft as a product of the prosecutors' imagination, he subsequently emphasized its nature as an almost globally shared set of beliefs (Ginzburg 1983, 1991). Methodologically, he was a main figure in microhistory and has signalled the importance of clues – apparently insignificant details, trivial phrases or gestures – and what they can reveal (*Clues, Myths, and the Historical*

Method, 1986). He has distinctive interests in art history and literary studies. He is an outspoken antagonist of postmodernism in history, while not infrequently being associated with it for resemblances in the style and subject matter of his writing (Serna and Pons 2000, 2005: 114–23; Pallares-Burke 2002: 184–211).

Jack Goody

Jack Goody (1919–) taught social anthropology at Cambridge. He is an anthropologist who has long explored the territories of history, for instance by studying the evolution of family structures and inheritance and, lately, the process of modernization. He conducted fieldwork in Ghana, and comparative research on food and flowers. Of vital importance are his contributions to the evaluation of the impact of literacy (see Chapter 4), a subject he has revisited in his *Myth, Ritual and the Oral* (2010) (Pallares-Burke 2002: 7–30).

Anthony Grafton

Anthony Grafton (1950–) is Professor of history at Princeton university. He is interested in the cultural history of Renaissance Europe as well as, with a broader chronology (from Antiquity), in the history of scholarship and education in the West, and in the history of science. He has written intellectual biographies of various Renaissance figures: Leon Batista Alberti, Girolamo Cardano and Joseph Scaliger. He has also paid attention to the history of the book, in such details as the footnote (Grafton 1997), or the laying out of texts in parallel columns during the third and fourth centuries (*Christianity and the Transformation of the Book*, 2006, with Megan Williams).

Antonio Gramsci

Antonio Gramsci (1891–1937) was a founder and early leader of the Italian Communist Party. Under the fascist regime, he was imprisoned and confined. Most of his writing comes from this period, is distinctively asystematic and was published posthumously: in his *Prison Notebooks* he was significantly concerned with Italian history; he also reflected on Marxist theory, and emphasized the influential role of intellectuals as well as cultural hegemony as a means by which capitalism maintained the status quo. Recent critical theorists have borrowed from him a number of concepts and terms (including 'subaltern classes', his way of referring to the dominated majority of society).

Stephen Greenblatt

Stephen Greenblatt (1943–) is a highly influential scholar who is credited with turning literary criticism into cultural poetics, an approach more closely related to history (see Chapter 3; Greenblatt 2005). He has taught literature and the humanities at the University of California, Berkeley and at Harvard. A part from his methodological contributions, his main areas of expertise are Shakespeare and Renaissance studies. Among others, he coined the successful notion of 'self-fashioning', which has frequently been taken to mean that individuals may shape themselves as they wish, but which he intended, more problematically, as being significantly limited by social constraint (*Renaissance Self-Fashioning*, 1980). Another key term that indicates his focus on the interaction between individuals and their cultures is 'negotiation'.

Aron J. Gurevich

Aron Jakovlevich Gurevich (1924–2006) was a prominent Russian medievalist of Jewish origin, who challenged the Marxist analysis of feudalism that was orthodoxy in the Soviet Union. His translated books and collections of essays include: *Categories of Medieval Culture* (1985), where he emphasizes the role of Christianity in the formation of the medieval world view; *Medieval Popular Culture: Problems of Belief and Perception* (1988), where he questions some of Bakhtin's interpretations; and *Historical Anthropology of the Middle Ages* (1992). He was appreciated abroad and close to the French historical school, and wrote *The Origins of European Individualism* (1995) at Jacques Le Goff's invitation (Mazour-Matusevich 2005).

Johan Huizinga

After initial training as an orientalist, Johan Huizinga (1872–1945) taught history at the universities of Groningen and Leiden. For his unfailing defence of freedom, he spent his last few years in Nazi imprisonment. In *The Autumn* (or *The Waning*) *of the Middle Ages* (1919), he portrayed a decadent European culture, in significant contrast to the image conveyed for the same period by Burckhardt's essay on the Renaissance. With *Homo Ludens* (1938), a milestone in leisure studies, he explored the play element of culture (Colie 1964; Roodenburg 2010).

Lynn Hunt

Lynn Hunt has taught at the University of California at Berkeley and Los Angeles. With *The New Cultural History* (ed., 1989, dedicated to

N. Z. Davis) she created the brand for a whole approach to history. Her areas of specialization include gender and the French Revolution (in *Liberty, Equality and Fraternity*, 2001, with Jack Censer, she offered a multimedia exploration of the Revolution). She adventured into psycho-history, for instance by investigating 'the collective, unconscious images of the familial order that underlie revolutionary politics' (Hunt 1992: xiii). In *Inventing Human Rights* (2007) she looked for the emotional prerequisites for the declaring of rights. In *Measuring Time, Making History* (2008) she reflected on modernity, time and how it matters for historians (on Hunt 2010, see Suggestions for further reading).

Lisa Jardine

Among her other positions and activities, Lisa Jardine (née Bronowski, 1944–) has taught in Cambridge and London (Queen Mary, where she also chairs the Centre for Editing Lives and Letters); she has sat on the councils and committees of several museums and institutions; she also frequently appears on TV and radio programmes on arts, history and current affairs. She has written on the scientific revolution and the early history of the Royal Society (*Ingenious Pursuits*, 1999), and researched the lives of Erasmus, Francis Bacon, Christopher Wren and Robert Hooke. She emphasized the power and wealth revealed (and global networks required) by Renaissance works of art (*Worldly Goods*, 1996) as well as the cultural interaction between seventeenth-century England and Holland (*Going Dutch*, 2008) (Snowman 2007: 221–31).

Ludmilla Jordanova

Ludmilla Jordanova (1949–) has taught in Cambridge (where she read natural sciences, developed an interest for the history and philosophy of science, and later directed the Centre for Research in the Arts, Social Sciences and Humanities) and London (King's). Her research interests include the history of science and medicine and its intersection with gender (*Nature Displayed*, 1999; *Sexual Visions*, 1989), portraiture (*Defining Features*, 2000) and public history. Her best-known book provides up-to-date and thought-provoking reflections on history as a discipline (Jordanova 2006).

Reinhart Koselleck

Reinhart Koselleck (1923–2006), a historian of the philosophy of the Enlightenment and of the economic development of the Prussian

Kingdom, taught theory of history at the University of Bielefeld in Germany and held frequent visiting positions in international research centres (among others, in Paris, New York and Chicago). He was the most prominent figure in the 'history of concepts' approach (see Chapter 3; Koselleck 2002) and a co-editor of *Geschichtliche Grundbegriffe* (Brunner *et al.* 1972–97).

Karl Lamprecht

In the 1890s, Karl Gotthard Lamprecht (1856–1915) was the protagonist, as the main target, of a methodological controversy (*Methodenstreit*) within the German historical establishment. His academic reputation was seriously damaged by the violent attacks of his opponents, who supported a narrow version of political history. While initially he was influential only among school teachers, the general public or abroad – his idea of *Volkseele* (collective psyche) has been seen as an anticipation of French *mentalité* – many of his preferences have become mainstream a century later, from his efforts towards an interdisciplinary cultural history to attempts to promote a world history (Chickering 1993; Daniel 2001: 210–16).

Juri M. Lotman

Juri Mikhailovich Lotman (1922–93), a Russian Jew, founded in Estonia the Tarku–Moscow semiotic school and became one of the most influential cultural and literary critics and theorists worldwide. He defined culture as a system of relationships between humans and the world, or as a dynamic repository of collective memory, and cultural semiotics as the study of the functional correlation of different sign systems. He also practised cultural history, particularly of the eighteenth-century Russian nobility (Lotman and Uspenskij 1984; Lotman 1997).

Alf Lüdtke

Alf Lüdtke (1943–), honorary Professor of the history of everyday life at the University of Erfurt, is the leading figure in the *Alltagsgeschichte* (Lüdtke 1995). He has studied state violence and the Prussian police in the nineteenth century; and workers' life experience and labour policies in the nineteenth and twentieth century. He is also interested in history as a discipline, and has contributed to challenging the objectivity of such practices as archiving and narrating (*Unsettling History*, 2010, ed. with Sebastian Jobs).

W. J. T. Mitchell

William J. Thomas Mitchell (1942–) is Professor of English and art history at the University of Chicago. He has pioneered the study of visual culture by recognizing an autonomous language and 'life' of images. With the book in which he introduced the notion of a pictorial turn, his aim was not only to describe the interactions of images and texts, 'but to trace their linkages to issues of power, value, and human interest' (Mitchell 1994: 5). His dialectic idea of how pictures work led him to define visuality as 'not just the social construction of vision, but the visual construction of the social' (Mitchell 2002: 179).

Pierre Nora

Pierre Nora (1931–) has had a distinguished career in publishing as well as history. At the Parisian house Gallimard, with the book series 'Bibliothèque des sciences humaines' and 'Bibliothèque des histoires', he was responsible for the circulation of hundreds of volumes, which often became highly influential in French culture. He played a major role as a public intellectual also by founding the journal *Le Débat*. In *Faire de l'historie* (1974, ed. with Jacques Le Goff; partially trans. as *Constructing the Past*, 1985) he co-edited an effective portrait of the state of the art in French historiography. The sites of memory (*lieux de memoire*) project (Nora 1996–98, 2001–10) remains his most remarkable legacy. Resulting from seminars at the EHESS, it is based on a dialectic notion of the relation between history and memory (history takes memory into account but is not reduced to it), on the conviction that symbols are socially constructed, and on a critical view of collective identities (Daileader and Whalen 2010: 440–60).

Erwin Panofsky

In the 1920s, Erwin Panofsky (1892–1968) belonged to the Hamburg circle of Warburg's library: from Ernst Cassirer he borrowed the notion of symbolic forms (Panofsky 1927, on linear perspective); with Fritz Saxl he wrote a seminal study of Dürer's *Melencolia I*. As a Jew, in 1934 he emigrated to the USA, where he joined the Institute of Advanced Study, Princeton. In his *Studies in Iconology* (1939) he argued for a distinction between iconography (recognizing the link between artistic motifs and conventional meaning) and iconology (interpreting the intrinsic significance of a work of art in the context of its underlying culture). An analysis of the parallels between *Gothic*

Architecture and Scholasticism (1951) is an example of his original model of an intellectual history of art (see www.dictionaryofarthistorians.org).

Armando Petrucci

Armando Petrucci (1932–) taught palaeography and diplomatics in Rome and at the Scuola Normale Superiore, Pisa, where he is Professor Emeritus. His interests cover the history of writing and of the book (with attention to the variety of texts, the materiality of their supporting media and their multiplicity of uses), of literacy (including its relevance in recent policies) and of libraries and scholarship. He enjoys an international reputation and has been particularly influential on the Spanish school of history of manuscript culture and of the book.

Daniel Roche

Daniel Roche (1935–) taught at the University of Paris and EHESS, and held the chair (now honorary) of the History of Enlightenment France at the Collège de France. He wrote his doctoral dissertation on the role of the French provincial academies in the dissemination of the Enlightenment. He studied *The People of Paris* (1981) and published the autobiography of an artisan (Ménétra 1986). His interests include the history of the book and reading, and urban history. In the field of the history of material culture, he examined – in collaborative research with his students – clothing as evidence of the attitudes and values of those wearing them (Roche 1994), and generally 'everyday things' (*choses banales*, Roche 2000). He has also produced a major study of travel 'mobility' (Roche 2003) (Pallares-Burke 2002: 106–28; Daileader and Whalen 2010: 513–26).

Lyndal Roper

Lyndal Roper (1956–) is an Australian historian with an interest in feminist theory, psychohistory and cultural studies. She has taught in London (Royal Holloway) and Oxford, where she co-edits the influential journal *Past and Present*. Under the supervision of Bob Scribner, she studied women and morals in Reformation Augsburg. She has subsequently worked on early modern witch-hunting, from the point of view of both its psychology (*Oedipus and the Devil*, 1994) and the historical background that may help explain its chronology and geography (*Witch Craze*, 2004) (Snowman 2007: 143–53).

Miri Rubin

Miri Rubin (1956–) was educated in Jerusalem and Cambridge, and has taught medieval and early modern history at Oxford and Queen Mary, University of London. Her main area of interest is represented by the religious cultures of late medieval Europe, which she studies in terms of social relations (charitable activities) and sacramental religion (the Eucharist), with attention to ritual and an anthropological approach to texts (such as anti-Jewish narratives) and images (on the Virgin Mary: *Emotion and Devotion*, 2009).

Marshall Sahlins

Marshall Sahlins (1930–) is Professor Emeritus of anthropology and of social sciences at the University of Chicago. He is interested in cultural evolution, and has studied the cultural specificity of economic systems. In his interpretation of early modern Pacific societies (particularly Fiji and Hawaii, as in the case of the death of Captain Cook, in controversy with Gananath Obyesekere) he has emphasized the distinction between indigenous cultures and Western rationality. His many books also encompass the concept of culture (*Culture and Practical Reason*, 1976) and the difference it can make to the writing of history (*Apologies to Thucydides*, 2004).

Raphael Samuel

Raphael Elkan Samuel (1934–96) was a historian and political activist of the British new left. At Oxford's Ruskin College he promoted history workshops, encouraging students to follow research projects built on their own experience; in 1976 he co-founded the *History Workshop Journal*, arguably the most dedicated platform for history from below. He practised oral and labour history and developed an interest in changing attitudes towards the past (*Theatres of Memory*, 1994) (G. Stedman Jones in *Oxford Dictionary of National Biography*).

Simon Schama

Educated in Cambridge, Simon Schama (1945–) has taught history and art history at Harvard and Columbia universities. He has produced and presented several BBC television series (including *A History of Britain*, 2000, surprisingly dominated by kings and battles), and is art and cultural critic for *The New Yorker*. As well as landscape and memory (see Chapter 4; Schama 1995), the genres and topics and of his books – written in a flamboyant literary style – include an interpretation of seventeenth-century Dutch culture (*The Embarrassment of Riches*, 1989; *Rembrandt's Eyes*, 1999); a sceptical chronicle of the French Revolution (*Citizens*, 1989), and tales of African Americans and the battles establishing that slavery was illegal in England (*Rough Crossings*, 2005). His most controversial publication connects two distant events by conscious 'unwarranted speculations' (*Dead Certainties*, 1991) (Snowman 2007: 256–66).

Joan Wallach Scott

Joan Wallach Scott (1941–), Professor at the School of Social Sciences at the Institute for Advanced Study in Princeton, is a historian of gender and a feminist theorist. From her initial competence as a labour historian, she developed a critique of the genealogy and use of notions such as 'class', which obscured the gender or racial constraints upon which they were built. She discussed the relationship between sexual equality and difference (*Only Paradoxes to Offer*, 1996; *Parité*, 2005), and has been critical of the way women's history is written, either subsumed under social forces or separate, in a disciplinary ghetto (Hughes-Warrington 2008: 308–16).

Bob Scribner

Born and educated in Sidney, Robert W. Scribner (1941–98), formerly reader in the social history of early modern Europe at Cambridge, has transformed our understanding of the German Reformation, which he intended as a process in which lay folk, as well as theologians, played an active role. His study of religious popular propaganda (Scribner 1994, first published in 1981), aware of cultural theory and anthropology, involved a major re-appreciation of the importance of visual and oral communication, along with print.

Quentin Skinner

Quentin Skinner (1940–) is Professor of the Humanities at Queen Mary, London, after having spent most of his academic life in Cambridge, where he was educated, taught political science and was later appointed Regius Professor of modern history. He is a major expert in the history of Western political thought, with particular interests in the republican tradition and the concept of liberty. Among other topics, he has studied the political thought of late medieval Italy, and Machiavelli, and has applied to Thomas Hobbes a concern with rhetoric, characteristic of his approach to intellectual history – a method for which he also repeatedly provided theoretical reflections (see Chapter 3; Pallares-Burke 2002: 212–40).

Peter Stearns

Peter N. Stearns was educated at Harvard and has taught at Carnegie Mellon and George Mason universities. He founded and edited the *Journal of Social History*. He has pioneered world history and – often in collaborative work – the history of emotions, with particular reference to modern North America (see Chapter 4), for instance by writing on sorrow, or on the construction of the twentieth-century emotional style of being 'cool' (Stearns 1994). He has also dealt with dieting and obesity, old age and work.

Keith Thomas

The Welsh historian Keith Thomas (1933–) taught history and the history of political thought at Oxford, as well as taking on responsibilities in many cultural institutions (including the Royal Historical Society, the British Academy, the National Gallery and the British Museum). He was inspired by Edward Evans-Pritchard's work on witchcraft, oracles and magic in Central Africa to develop a historical anthropology of beliefs in early modern England (Thomas 1971). He has subsequently studied changing attitudes towards animals and nature (Thomas 1983) and, more recently, roads of fulfilment in early modern England (*The Ends of Life*, 2009). His shorter essays cover many other topics, including attitudes to laughter, or cleanliness and godliness (Pallares-Burke 2002: 80–105).

E. P. Thompson

After World War II, the British historian Edward Palmer Thompson (1924–93) founded, with Christopher Hill, Eric Hobsbawm and others, the Communist Party Historians Group. He remained throughout his life an intellectual in the Marxist tradition – studying the activities of ordinary people in eighteenth- and nineteenth-century England – and an activist, particularly in the pacifist movement, together with his wife Dorothy, herself a historian. He wrote biographies of William Morris (1955) and William Blake (1993). In his influential *The Making of the*

English Working Class (1963), he defined class as a relationship that changed over time; in his view, the development of class-consciousness owed much to various traditions and to the workers' agency, in the light of moral choice and values (Hughes-Warrington 2008: 346–54; J. Rule in *Oxford Dictionary of National Biography*).

Aby Warburg

The London institute named after Aby Warburg (1866–1929) derives from the research library he set up in early twentieth-century Hamburg, with the assistance of Fritz Saxl and Gertrud Bing; its interdisciplinary character and thematic arrangement still make it a unique place of study. Warburg's interests included psychology and anthropology (with a fieldtrip to the Navaho and Pueblo West in 1895). His original research aimed at discerning classical mythology and symbolism in postclassical art. A fascination with memory led him to plan *Mnemosyne*, an image atlas, with panels graphically displaying the conceptual relationships between pictures. Gombrich wrote Warburg's standard intellectual biography (www.dictionaryofarthistorians.org).

Hayden White

Formerly Professor of comparative literature at Stanford, Hayden White (1928–) is Emeritus Professor of the history of consciousness at the University of California, Santa Cruz. Continuing his controversial investigation of the rhetorical forms of the historical discourse (White 1973; see Chapter 2; also *Tropics of Discourse*, 1978), he has explored the notion of authority in art and literature and the problems of meaning in different epochs (*The Content of the Form*, 1987), as well as the treatment of history in recent literary criticism (*Figurative Realism*, 1997) (Hughes-Warrington 2008: 388–95).

Raymond Williams

Raymond Williams (1921–88) was a Welsh cultural and literary critic, whose work laid the foundation for the British tradition of cultural studies. His *Culture and Society* (Williams 1958) mapped a change in the notion of culture, which in response to the industrial revolution came to mean 'a whole way of life, material, intellectual and spiritual'. In *The Long Revolution* (1961), he claimed that – with the growth of the popular press, of standard English and of the reading public – the West had witnessed a cultural revolution, along with the democratic and the industrial ones (D. Smith in *Oxford Dictionary of National Biography*).

Theodore Zeldin

Theodore Zeldin (1933–) is an internationally famous English intellectual, who started his academic career as a historian of France. His major study of nineteenth- and twentieth-century France centres on such unusual issues as ambition, love, interest and taste (*A History of French Passions*, two volumes, 1973–77). He subsequently moved away from history strictly speaking, to explore the preoccupations of ordinary people around the world (*An Intimate History of Humanity*, 1994) and to promote an improvement in personal and work relations (Snowman 2007: 50–61).

Notes

1 This list is intended to complement the text, providing a minimum of additional information, and connecting data that may be located in different sections of the book. Consequently, to avoid duplication, it excludes a few scholars whose career and intellectual contribution, or at least relevance to our subject matter, is reasonably portrayed and discussed in the main text, within the space constraints of a book of this size (among them T. S. Kuhn, A. O. Lovejoy, D. F. McKenzie and H. M. McLuhan). To find the relevant passages, the reader will need to use the index. It goes without saying that this list comprises people who differ significantly from one another in their specialization or orientation. Works mentioned only in this appendix are simply cited by title and year of first publication, without full bibliographical information. (Also, in this section only, the date is that of publication in the original language, unless specific bibliographic reference to an English translation is given.) Reference to discussions of their work by others is limited, occasionally suggesting texts where the reader can find a wider illustration of their life and work.

Bibliography

Adler, K. (2002) 'The History of Science, Or, An Oxymoronic Theory of Relativistic Objectivity', in L. Kramer and S. Maza (eds) *A Companion to Western Historical Thought*, Oxford: Blackwell, pp. 296–318.

Amelang, J. S. (1998) *The Flight of Icarus: Artisan autobiography in early modern Europe*, Stanford, CA: Stanford University Press.

Anderson, B. (1991) *Imagined Communities: Reflections on the origin and spread of nationalism*, revised edn, London: Verso.

Ariès, P. (1996) *Centuries of Childhood* [1962], trans. R. Baldick, London: Pimlico.

——(1988) 'Histoire des mentalités', in J. Le Goff (ed.) *La nouvelle histoire*, new edn, Brussels: Complexe, pp. 167–90.

Ariès, P. and Duby, G. (general eds) (1987–91) *A History of Private Life*, five volumes, Cambridge, MA/London: Belknap Press of Harvard University Press.

Austin, J. L. (1975) *How to Do Things with Words*, 2nd edn, Oxford: Clarendon.

Bachelard, G. (1988) *Air and Dreams: An essay on the imagination of movement* [1943], trans. E. R. Farrell and C. F. Farrell, Dallas: Dallas Institute of Humanities and Culture.

Bakhtin, M. M. (1984) *Rabelais and His World*, trans. H. Iswolsky, new edn, Bloomington, IN: Indiana University Press [translation originally published 1968].

Badinter, E. (1981) *The Myth of Motherhood: An historical view of the maternal instinct*, London: Souvenir.

Barnard, A. (2011) *Social Anthropology and Human Origins*, Cambridge: Cambridge University Press.

Barthes, R. (1977) 'The Death of the Author', in R. Barthes, *Image Music Text*, ed. and trans. S. Heath, London: Fontana, pp. 142–48.

Baudrillard, J. (1998) *The Consumer Society: Myths and structures* [1970], London: Sage.

——(2005) *The System of Objects* [1968], trans. J. Benedict, London/New York: Verso.

Baxandall, M. (1971) *Giotto and the Orators: Humanist observers of painting in Italy and the discovery of pictorial composition, 1350–1450*, Oxford: Clarendon.

——(1988) *Painting and Experience in Fifteenth-Century Italy: A primer in the social history of pictorial style*, 2nd edn, Oxford: Oxford University Press.

Behringer, W. (2010) *A Cultural History of Climate*, Cambridge: Polity.

Bell, D. A. (2002) 'Total History and Microhistory: The French and Italian Paradigms', in L. Kramer and S. Maza (eds) *A Companion to Western Historical Thought*, Oxford: Blackwell, pp. 262–76.

Bénéton, P. (1975) *Histoire de mots: culture et civilisation*, Paris: Fondation nationale des sciences politiques.

Bentley, J. H. (2002) 'The New World History', in L. Kramer and S. Maza (eds) *A Companion to Western Historical Thought*, Oxford: Blackwell, pp. 393–416.

Bloch, M. (1973) *The Royal Touch: Sacred monarchy and scrofula in England and France*, trans. J. E. Anderson, London: Routledge.

——(1989) *The Feudal Society*, trans. L. A. Manyon, 2nd edn, London: Routledge.

——(1992) *The Historian's Craft*, trans. P. Putnam, Manchester, UK: Manchester University Press.

Blondel, C. (1926) *La mentalité primitive*, Paris: Stock.

Boia, L. (1998) *Pour une histoire de l'imaginaire*, Paris: Les Belles Lettres.

——(2004) *Forever Young: A cultural history of longevity*, London: Reaktion Books.

——(2005) *The Weather in the Imagination*, London: Reaktion Books.

Boswell, J. (1980) *Christianity, Social Tolerance, and Homosexuality: Gay people in Western Europe from the beginning of the Christian era to the fourteenth century*, Chicago, IL/London: University of Chicago Press.

——(1988) *The Kindness of Strangers: The abandonment of children in Western Europe from Late Antiquity to the Renaissance*, London: Penguin.

Bots, H. and Waquet, F. (1997) *La République des lettres*, Paris: Belin.

Bouwsma, W. J. (2000) *The Waning of the Renaissance, 1550–1640*, New Haven, CT/London: Yale University Press.

Bouza, F. (2001) *Corre manuscrito: una historia cultural del Siglo de Oro*, Madrid: Pons.

Boyd, K. (ed.) (1999) *Encyclopedia of Historians and Historical Writing*, London/Chicago, IL: Fitzroy Dearborn.

Bremmer, J. and Roodenburg, H. (eds) (1991) *A Cultural History of Gesture: From Antiquity to the present day*, Cambridge: Polity.

Brett, A. (2002) 'What is Intellectual History Now?', in D. Cannadine (ed.) *What Is History Now?*, Basingstoke, UK: Palgrave Macmillan, pp. 113–31.

Brewer, J. (1997) *The Pleasures of the Imagination: English culture in the eighteenth century*, London: HarperCollins.

——(2004) 'Il tempo minimo. Storia culturale e vita quotidiana', *Studi culturali*, 1: 7–30.

——(2010) 'Microhistory and the Histories of Everyday Life', *Cultural and Social History*, 7: 87–109.

Briggs, A. and Burke, P. (2005) *A Social History of the Media: From Gutenberg to the Internet*, 2nd edn, Cambridge: Polity.

Brown, P. (1988) *The Body and Society: Men, women and sexual renunciation in early Christianity*, New York: Columbia University Press.

Brunner, O., Conze, W. and Koselleck, R. (eds) (1972–97) *Geschichtliche Grundbegriffe. Historisches Lexikon zur politisch-sozialer Sprache in Deutschland*, eight volumes, Stuttgart: Klett-Cotta.

Bryson, N. (1992) 'Art in context', in R. Cohen (ed.) *Studies in Historical Change*, Charlottesville, VA: University of Virginia Press, pp. 18–42.

Bryson, N., Holly, M. A. and Moxey, K. (eds) (1994) *Visual Culture: Images and interpretations*, Hanover, NH: University Press of New England.

Burckhardt, J. (1943) *Reflections on History*, trans. M. D. Hottinger, London: G. Allen & Unwin.

——(1990) *The Civilization of the Renaissance in Italy* [1860], trans. S. G. C. Middlemore, London: Penguin.

——(1998) *The Greeks and Greek Civilization*, trans. S. Stern, London: HarperCollins.

——(2002) *History of Greek Culture*, trans. P. Hilty, Mineola, NY: Dover.

Burguière, A. (1982) 'The Fate of the History of *Mentalités* in the *Annales*', *Comparative Studies in Society and History*, 24: 424–37.

——(1986) 'Anthropologie historique', in A. Burguière (ed.) *Dictionnaire des sciences historiques*, Paris: PUF, pp. 52–60.

——(2009) *The Annales School: An intellectual history*, trans. J. M. Todd, Ithaca, NY: Cornell University Press.

Burke, P. (1972) *Culture and Society in Renaissance Italy, 1420–1540*, London: Batsford (2nd edn, 1986).

——(ed.) (1973) *A New Kind of History from the Writings of Febvre*, trans. K. Folca, London: Routledge & Kegan Paul.

——(1980) *Sociology and History*, London: Allen & Unwin.

——(1990) *The French Historical Revolution: The* Annales *School, 1929–89*, Cambridge: Polity.

——(1997) 'Strengths and Weaknesses of the History of Mentalities', in *Varieties of Cultural History*, Cambridge: Polity, pp. 172–82.

——(2000) *A Social History of Knowledge: From Gutenberg to Diderot*, Cambridge: Polity.

——(2001a) *Eyewitnessing: The uses of images as historical evidence*, London: Reaktion Books.

——(2001b) 'History of Events and the Revival of Narrative', in P. Burke (ed.) *New Perspectives on Historical Writing*, 2nd edn, Cambridge: Polity, pp. 283–300.

——(2001c) 'Overture. The New History: Its Past and its Future', in P. Burke (ed.) *New Perspectives on Historical Writing*, op. cit., pp. 1–24.

——(2004a) 'History and Folklore: A Historiographical Survey', *Folklore*, 115: 133–39, www.findarticles.com/p/articles/mi_m2386/is_2_115/ai_n8693724.

——(2004b) *Languages and Communities in Early Modern Europe*, Cambridge: Cambridge University Press.

——(2005) *History and Social Theory*, 2nd edn, Cambridge: Polity [first published 1992].

——(2007) 'Freud and Cultural History', *Psychoanalysis and History*, 9: 5–15.

——(2008a) 'The Invention of Microhistory', *Rivista di storia economica*, 24: 259–73.

——(2008b) *What is Cultural History?*, 2nd edn, Cambridge: Polity.

——(2009a) *Cultural Hybridity*, Cambridge: Polity.

——(2009b) *Popular Culture in Early Modern Europe*, 3rd edn, Farnham: Ashgate.

——(2010a) 'Interrogating the Eyewitness', *Cultural and Social History*, 7: 435–44.

——(2010b) 'Polyphonic History', *Arbor*, CLXXXVI–743: 479–86, http://arbor.revistas.csic.es/index.php/arbor/article/view/815/822.

Butler, J. (1990) *Gender Trouble. Feminism and subversion of identity*, New York/London: Routledge.

——(1993) *Bodies That Matter. On the discursive limits of 'sex'*, New York/London: Routledge.

Bynum, C. W. (1987) *Holy Feast and Holy Fast: The Religious Significance of Food to Medieval Women*, Berkeley/Los Angeles, CA: University of California Press.

Calaresu, M., De Vivo, F. and Rubiés, J.-P. (eds) (2010) *Exploring Cultural History: Essays in Honour of Peter Burke*, Farnham: Ashgate.

Caro Baroja, J. (1964) *The World of the Witches*, trans. N. Glendinning, London: Weidenfeld & Nicolson.

——(1965) *El carnaval: análisis histórico-cultural*, Madrid: Taurus.

Carr, E. H. (2001) *What is History?*, with a new introduction by R. J. Evans, Basingstoke, UK: Palgrave Macmillan.

Castillo Gómez, A. (2006) *Entre la pluma y la pared. Una historia de la cultura escritra en los Siglos de Oro*, Madrid: Akal.

de Certeau, M. (1980) 'Writing vs Time: History and Anthropology in the works of Lafitau', trans. J. Hovde, *Yale French Studies*, 59: 37–64.

——(1984) *The Practice of Everyday Life*, Berkeley, CA: University of California Press.

——(1986) *Heterologies: Discourse on the Other*, trans. B. Massoumi, Manchester, UK: Manchester University Press.

Chartier, R. (1986) 'Images', in A. Burguière (ed.) *Dictionnaire des sciences historiques*, Paris: PUF, pp. 345–47.

——(1991) *The Cultural Origins of the French Revolution*, trans. L. G. Cochrane, Durham, NC: Duke University Press.

——(1994) *The Order of Books: Readers, authors, and libraries in Europe between the fourteenth and eighteenth centuries*, trans. L. G. Cochrane, Cambridge: Polity.

——(1995) *Forms and Meaning: Texts, performances, and audiences from codex to computer*, Philadelphia, PA: University of Pennsylvania Press.

——(1996) 'L'histoire culturelle', in J. Revel and N. Wachtel (eds) *Une école pour les sciences sociales*, Paris: Éditions du Cerf-Éditions de l'ÉHÉSS, pp. 73–92.

——(1997) *On the Edge of the Cliff: History, language, and practices*, trans. L. G. Cochrane, Baltimore, MD/London: Johns Hopkins University Press.

——(1999a) 'The World as Representation' [1989], in J. Revel and L. Hunt (eds) *Histories: French constructions of the past*, trans. A. Goldhammer *et al.*, New York: New Press, pp. 544–58.

——(1999b) *Publishing Drama in Early Modern Europe*, London: British Library.

——(2001) 'Cultural History', in N. J. Smelser and P. B. Baltes (eds) *International Encyclopedia of the Social & Behavioral Sciences*, Amsterdam/Oxford: Elsevier, pp. 3075–81.

——(2007) *Inscription and Erasure: Literature and written culture from the eleventh to the eighteenth century*, trans. A. Goldhammer, Philadelphia, PA: University of Pennsylvania Press.

Chickering, R. (1993) *Karl Lamprecht: A German academic life (1856–1915)*, Atlantic Highlands, NJ: Humanities Press.

Christiansen, P. O. (2000) *Kulturhistorie som opposition: træk af forskellige fagtraditioner*, Copenhagen: Samleren.

——(2008) 'L'Experience et la vie quotidienne: L'histoire culturelle en Scandinavie', trans. J. P. Durix, in Poirrier, P. (ed.) *L'Histoire culturelle: un 'tournant mondial' dans l'historiographie?*, Dijon: Editions Universitaires de Dijon, pp. 65–78 (2010 Italian edn, trans. A. Arcangeli, pp. 223–48).

Cipolla, C. M. (1965) *Guns and Sails in the Early Phase of European Expansion, 1400–1700*, London: Collins.

——(1967) *Clocks and Culture, 1300–1700*, London: Collins.

Clark, E. A. (2004) *History, Theory, Text: Historians and the linguistic turn*, Cambridge, MA: Harvard University Press.

Clark, S. (1997) *Thinking with Demons: The idea of witchcraft in early modern Europe*, Oxford: Clarendon.

——(2007) *Vanities of the Eye: Vision in early modern European culture*, Oxford: Oxford University Press.

Classen, C. (1993) *Worlds of Sense: Exploring the senses in history and across cultures*, London: Routledge.

Cohen, Y. (2010) 'Les jeunes en France: naissance et construction d'une identité sociale. Essai d'historiographie', *Storica*, 46: 9–47.

Colie, R. (1964) 'Johan Huizinga and the Task of Cultural History', *American Historical Review*, 69: 607–30.

Colley, L. (2007) *The Ordeal of Elizabeth Marsh: A woman in world history*, London: HarperPress.

Corbin, A. (1986) *The Foul and the Fragrant: Odor and the French social imagination*, trans. M. K. Berg, Leamington Spa, UK: Berg.

——(1995) *Time, Desire, and Horror: Towards a history of the senses*, trans. J. Birrell, Cambridge: Polity.

Corbin, A., Courtine, J.-J. and Vigarello, G. (eds) (2005–06) *Histoire du corps*, three volumes, Paris: Seuil.

Courtine, J.-J. and Haroche, C. (1994) *Histoire du visage*, Paris: Payot & Rivage.

Crary, J. (1990) *Techniques of the Observer: On vision and modernity in the nineteenth century*, Cambridge, MA/London: MIT Press.

Curtis, N. (ed.) (2010) *The Pictorial Turn*, London: Routledge.

Daileader, P. and Whalen, P. (eds) (2010) *French Historians 1900–2000: New historical writing in twentieth-century France*, Chichester, UK: Wiley-Blackwell.

Daniel, U. (2001) *Kompendium Kulturgeschichte. Theorien, Praxis, Schlüsselwörter*, Frankfurt: Suhrkamp (Spanish trans. Madrid: Alianza, 2005).

Darnton, R. (1984) 'Workers revolt: the great cat massacre of the rue Saint-Séverin', in *The Great Cat Massacre and Other Episodes in French Cultural History*, New York: Basic Books, pp. 75–104.

——(1995) 'Diffusion vs. Discourse: Conceptual Shifts in Intellectual History and the Historiography of the French Revolution', in C. Barros (ed.) *A Historia a Debate*, Actas del Congreso Internacional, Santiago de Compostela-A Coruña (7–11 julio 1993), Vol. 2, *Retorno del sujeto*, pp. 179–92.

——(2000) 'Presidential Address: An Early Information Society. News and the Media in Eighteenth-Century Paris', *American Historical Review*, 105: 1–35, www.historycooperative.org/journals/ahr/105.1/ah000001.html.

Daston, L. (ed.) (2004) *Things that Talk: Object lessons from art and science*, New York: Zone Books.

Davis, N. Z. (1983) *The Return of Martin Guerre*, Cambridge, MA/London: Harvard University Press.

——(1987) *Fiction in the Archives: Pardon tales and their tellers in sixteenth-century France*, Stanford, CA: Stanford University Press.

——(1990) 'The Shapes of Social History', *Storia della storiografia*, 17: 28–34.

——(1995) *Women on the Margins: Three seventeenth-century lives*, Cambridge, MA/London: Harvard University Press.

——(2000) *The Gift in Sixteenth-Century France*, Oxford: Oxford University Press.

——(2006) *Trickster Travels: A sixteenth-century Muslim between worlds*, New York: Hill & Wang.

Debord, G. (1994) *The Society of the Spectacle* [1967], New York: Zone.

Decharneux, B. and Nefontaine, L. (1998) *Le Symbole*, Paris: Presses Universitaires de France.

del Río Barredo, M. J. (2010) 'Historia y teoría. Notas para un estudio de la obra de Peter Burke', in P. Burke, *Hibridismo cultural*, trans. S. Chaparro Martínez, Madrid: Akal, pp. 5–57.

Dikovitskaya, M. (2005) *Visual Culture: The study of the visual after the cultural turn*, Cambridge, MA/London: MIT Press.

Dixon, T. (2003) *From Passions to Emotions: The creation of a secular psychological category*, Cambridge: Cambridge University Press.

Down, L. L. (2010) *Writing Gender History*, 2nd edn, London: Bloomsbury Academic.

Duara, P. (2002) 'Postcolonial History', in L. Kramer and S. Maza (eds) *A Companion to Western Historical Thought*, Oxford: Blackwell, pp. 417–31.

Duby, G. (1961) 'Histoire des mentalités', in C. Samaran (ed.) *L'Histoire et ses méthodes*, Paris: Gallimard, pp. 937–66.

——(1980) *The Three Orders: Feudal society imagined*, trans. A. Goldhammer, Chicago, IL/London: University of Chicago Press.

Duby, G. and Mandrou, R. (1965) *A History of French Civilization*, trans. J. B. Atkinson, London: Weidenfeld & Nicolson.

Duby, G. and Perrot, M. (general eds) (1992–94) *A History of Women in the West*, five volumes, Cambridge, MA/London: Belknap Press of Harvard University Press.

Eisenstein, E. L. (1979) *The Printing Press as an Agent of Change: Communications and cultural transformations in early-modern Europe*, two volumes, Cambridge: Cambridge University Press.

——(1993) *The Printing Revolution in Early Modern Europe*, 2nd edn, Cambridge: Cambridge University Press.

Eley, G. (2005) *A Crooked Line: From cultural history to the history of society*, Ann Arbor, MI: University of Michigan Press.

Elias, N. (1994) *The Civilizing Process* [1939], trans. E. Jephcott, rev. edn, Oxford: Blackwell (part I, 'The history of manners', originally published as a separate volume).

——(2006) *The Court Society* [1969], trans. E. Jephcott, rev. edn, Dublin: University College Dublin Press (The collected works of Norbert Elias, II).

Elias, N. and Dunning, E. (1986) *The Quest for Excitement: Sport and leisure in the civilizing process*, Oxford: Blackwell.

Evans, J. and Hall, S. (eds) (1999) *Visual Culture: The reader*, London: Sage.

Evergates, T. (1997) 'The Feudal imaginary of Georges Duby', *Journal of Medieval and Early Modern Studies*, 27: 641–60.

Falcon, F. (2002) *História cultural: uma nova visão sobre a sociedade e a cultura*, Rio de Janeiro: Campus.

Farge, A. (1993) *Fragile Lives: Violence, power and solidarity in eighteenth-century Paris*, trans. C. Shelton, Cambridge: Polity.

Febvre, L. (1937) 'Une Encyclopédie française: pourquoi, comment?', in *Encyclopédie française*, 1, pp. 1.04.11–14.

——(1982) *The Problem of Unbelief in the Sixteenth Century: The religion of Rabelais*, trans. B. Gottlieb, Cambridge, MA/London: Harvard University Press.

Fernández-Armesto, F. (1997) *Truth: A History and a Guide for the Perplexed*, London: Bantam.

——(2001) *Food: A history*, London: Macmillan.

——(2002) 'Epilogue: What is History Now?', in D. Cannadine (ed.) *What Is History Now?*, Basingstoke, UK: Palgrave Macmillan, pp. 148–61.

——(2004) *So You Think You Are Human? A brief history of humankind*, Oxford: Oxford University Press.

——(2006) *Pathfinders: A global history of exploration*, Oxford: Oxford University Press.

Foucault, M. (1973) 'The Discourse on Language', trans. R. Swyer, in M. Foucault, *The Archaeology of Knowledge*, trans. A. M. Sheridan Smith, New York: Pantheon, pp. 215–37.

——(1977a) *Discipline and Punish: The birth of the prison*, trans. A. Sheridan, London: Allen Lane.

——(1977b) 'What is an Author?', in M. Foucault, *Language, Counter-Memory, Practice*, ed. D. F. Bouchard, trans. D. F. Bouchard and S. Simon, Ithaca, NY: Cornell University Press, pp. 113–38 (a different translaton by J. V. Harrari is available in *The Foucault Reader*, ed. P. Rabinow, New York: Pantheon Books, 1984, pp. 101–20).

——(1979–88) *The History of Sexuality*, trans. R. Hurley, three volumes, London: Allen Lane.

——(2002) *The Order of Things: An archaeology of the human sciences*, London: Routledge.

——(2003) *Abnormal: Lectures at the Collège de France, 1974–1975*, eds V. Marchetti and A. Salomoni, trans. G. Burchell, London: Verso.

——(2006) *History of Madness* [1961], ed. J. Khalfa, trans. J. Murphy and J. Khalfa, London/New York: Routledge.

Freedberg, D. (1989) *The Power of Images: Studies in the history and theory of response*, Chicago, IL: University of Chicago Press.

Frijhoff, W. (2007) *Fulfilling God's Mission: The two worlds of Dominie Everardus Bogardus, 1607–1647*, trans. M. Heerspink Scholz, Leiden: Brill.

——(2010) 'Michel de Certeau (1925–86)', in P. Daileader and P. Whalen (eds) *French Historians 1900–2000: New historical writing in twentieth-century France*, Chichester, UK: Wiley-Blackwell, pp. 77–92.

Frykman, J. and Löfgren, O. (1987) *Culture Builders: A historical anthropology of middle-class life*, trans. A. Crozier, New Brunswick, NJ/London: Rutgers University Press.

Gabaccia, D. R. (2002) 'The Multicultural History of Nations', in L. Kramer and S. Maza (eds) *A Companion to Western Historical Thought*, Oxford: Blackwell, pp. 432–46.

Galison, P. (2003) *Einstein's Clocks, Poincaré's Maps: Empires of time*, London: Sceptre.

Gaskell, I. (2001) 'Visual History', in P. Burke (ed.) *New Perspectives on Historical Writing*, 2nd edn, Cambridge: Polity, pp. 187–217.

Gay, P. (1985) *Freud for Historians*, New York/Oxford: Oxford University Press.

Geertz, C. (1973) *The Interpretation of Cultures: Selected essays*, New York: Basic Books.

Gentilcore, D. (2002) 'The Subcultures of the Renaissance World', in G. Ruggiero (ed.) *A Companion to the Worlds of the Renaissance*, Oxford: Blackwell, pp. 299–315.

——(2005) 'Anthropological Approaches', in G. Walker (ed.) *Writing Early Modern History*, London: Hodder Arnold, pp. 49–70.

Gergen, K. J. (1998) 'History and Psychology: Three weddings and a future', in P. N. Stearns and J. Lewis (eds) *An Emotional History of the United States*, New York: New York University Press, pp. 15–29.

Gil, J. (2010) 'Sobre los límites de la rapresentación', *Arbor*, CLXXXVI–743: 461–65, http://arbor.revistas.csic.es/index.php/arbor/article/view/813/820.

Ginzburg, C. (1980) *The Cheese and the Worms: The cosmos of a sixteenth-century miller*, trans. J. and A. Tedeschi, London: Routledge & Kegan Paul.

——(1983) *The Night Battles: Witchcraft and agrarian cults in the sixteenth and seventeenth centuries*, trans. J. and A. Tedeschi, London: Routledge & Kegan Paul.

——(1991) *Ecstasies: Decipering the witches' Sabbath*, trans. R. Rosenthal, Harmondsworth, UK: Penguin.

Gombrich, E. H. (1969) *In Search of Cultural History*, Oxford: Clarendon.

Goody, J. (1977) *The Domestication of the Savage Mind*, Cambridge: Cambridge University Press.

——(1986) *The Logic of Writing and the Organization of Society*, Cambridge: Cambridge University Press.

Goudsblom, J. (1992) *Fire and Civilization*, London: Allen Lane.

Grafton, A. (1997) *The Footnote: A curious history*, London: Faber.

Grassby, R. (2005) 'Material Culture and Cultural History', *Journal of Interdisciplinary History*, 35: 591–603.

Green, A. (2008) *Cultural History*, Basingstoke, UK: Palgrave.

Greenblatt, S. (1991) *Marvelous Possessions. The Wonder of the New World*, Oxford: Clarendon.

——(2005) *The Greenblatt Reader*, ed. M. Payne, Oxford: Blackwell.

——(2010) *Cultural Mobility: A Manifesto*, Cambridge: Cambridge University Press.

Groebner, V. (2007) *Who are You? Identification, deception, and surveillance in early modern Europe*, trans. M. Kyburz and J. Peck, New York: Zone.

Gunn, S. (2006) *History and Cultural Theory*, Harlow: Longman.

Havelock, E. A. (1986) *Muse Learns to Write: Reflections on orality and literacy from antiquity to the present*, New Haven, CT: Yale University Press.

Hegel, G. W. F. (1975) *Lectures on the Philosophy of World History: Introduction*, trans. H. B. Nisbet, Cambridge: Cambridge University Press.

Hinde, J. R. (2000) *Jacob Burckhardt and the Crisis of Modernity*, Montreal and Kingston: McGill-Queen's University Press.

Hobsbawm, E. and Ranger, T. (eds) (1983) *The Invention of Tradition*, Cambridge: Cambridge University Press.

Howells, R. (2003) *Visual Culture*, Cambridge: Polity.

Hufton, O. (2002) 'What is Religious History Now?', in D. Cannadine (ed.) *What Is History Now?*, Basingstoke, UK: Palgrave Macmillan, pp. 57–79.

Hughes, J. D. (2006) *What is Environmental History?*, Cambridge: Polity.

Hughes-Warrington, M. (2008) *Fifty Key Thinkers on History*, 2nd edn, London: Routledge.

Huizinga, J. (1970) 'The task of cultural history', in *Men and Ideas: History, the Middle Ages, the Renaissance*, trans. J. S. Holmes and H. van Marle, New York: Harper & Row, pp. 17–76.

Hunt, L. (1992) *The Family Romance of the French Revolution*, Berkeley/Los Angeles, CA: University of California Press.

——(2002) 'Psychology, Psychoanalysis, and Historical Thought', in L. Kramer and S. Maza (eds) *A Companion to Western Historical Thought*, Oxford: Blackwell, pp. 337–56.

——(2010) *La storia culturale nell'età globale*, Pisa: Edizioni ETS.

Jardine, N., Secord, J. A. and Spary, A. C. (eds) (1996) *Cultures of Natural History*, Cambridge: Cambridge University Press.

Jarrick, A. (1999) *Back to Modern Reason*, Liverpool, UK: Liverpool University Press.

Jay, M. (1993) *Downcast Eyes: The denigration of vision in twentieth-century French thought*, Berkeley, CA/London: University of California Press.

Jenkins, K. (1997) *The Postmodern History Reader*, London: Routledge.

Jenks, C. (ed.) (1995) *Visual Culture*, London: Routledge.

Jordanova, L. (2006) *History in Practice*, 2nd edn, London: Hodder Arnold.

Jütte, R. (2004) *A History of the Senses: From antiquity to cyberspace*, Cambridge: Polity.

Kalof, L. and Bynum, W. (eds) (2010) *A Cultural History of the Human Body*, six volumes, Oxford: Berg.

Kantorowicz, E. H. (1997) *The King's Two Bodies: A study in mediaeval political theology* [1957], Princeton, NJ: Princeton University Press.

Kessler-Harris, A. (2002) 'What is Gender History Now?', in D. Cannadine (ed.) *What Is History Now?*, Basingstoke, UK: Palgrave Macmillan, pp. 95–112.

Koselleck, R. (1985) *Futures Past: On the semantics of historical time*, trans. K. Tribe, Cambridge, MA/London: MIT Press.

——(1994) 'Some Reflections on the Temporal Structure of Conceptual Change', in W. Melching and W. Velema (eds) *Main Trends in Cultural History*, Amsterdam/Atlanta, GA: Rodopi, pp. 7–15.

——(2002) *The Practice of Conceptual History: Timing history, spacing concepts*, Stanford, CA: Stanford University Press.

Kuhn, T. S. (1957) *The Copernican Revolution: Planetary astronomy in the development of Western thought*, Cambridge, MA: Harvard University Press.

——(1970) *The Structure of Scientific Revolutions*, 2nd edn, Chicago, IL/London: University of Chicago Press.

Landwehr, A. (2008) *Historische Diskursanalyse*, Frankfurt: Campus.

Landwehr, A. and Stockhorst, S. (2004) *Einführung in die Europäische Kulturgeschichte*, Paderborn: Schöningh.

Laneyrie-Dagen, N. (1997) *L'invention du corps: la représentation de l'homme du Moyen Âge à la fin du xix siècle*, Paris: Flammarion.

Laqueur, T. W. (2000) *Making Sex: Body and gender from the Greeks to Freud*, Cambridge, MA: Harvard University Press.

——(2003) *Solitary Sex: A cultural history of masturbation*, New York: Zone.

Le Goff, J. (1985) 'Mentalities: a history of ambiguities', trans. D. Denby, in J. Le Goff and P. Nora (eds) *Constructing the Past: Essays in historical methodology*, Cambridge: Cambridge University Press; Paris: Editions de la Maison des Sciences de l'Homme, pp. 166–80.

Le Roy Ladurie, E. (1978) *Montaillou: Cathars and Catholics in a French village, 1294–1324*, trans. B. Bray, London: Scolar Press.

Levi, G. (1985) 'I pericoli del Geertzismo', *Quaderni Storici*, 20: 269–77.

——(2001) 'On microhistory', in P. Burke (ed.) *New Perspectives on Historical Writing*, 2nd edn, Cambridge: Polity, pp. 97–119.

Lévy-Bruhl, L. (1923) *Primitive Mentality*, trans. L. A. Clare, London: G. Allen & Unwin; New York: Macmillan.

Lotman, Ju. M. (1997) *Russlands Adel: eine Kulturgeschichte von Peter I bis Nikolaus I*, Vienna: Böhlau.

Lotman, Ju. M. and Uspenskij, B. A. (1984) *The Semiotics of Russian Culture*, ed. A. Shukman, Ann Arbor: University of Michigan.

Love, H. (1993) *Scribal Publication in Seventeenth-Century England*, Oxford: Clarendon.

Lovejoy, A. O. (1970) *The Great Chain of Being: A study of the history of an idea*, Cambridge, MA: Harvard University Press.

Lüdtke, A. (ed.) (1995) *The History of Everyday Life: Reconstructing historical experiences and ways of life*, trans. W. Templer, Princeton, NJ: Princeton University Press.

Lung, E. (2009) *Istorie culturală. Origini, evoluţii, tendinţe*, Bucharest: Editura Universităţii din Bucureşti.

Lutter, C. and Reisenleitner, M. (1998) *Cultural Studies: eine Einführung*, Vienna: Turia & Kant (Italian trans. Milan: B. Mondadori, 2004).

Lyotard, J.-F. (1984) *The Postmodern Condition*, trans. G. Bennington and B. Massumi, Manchester, UK: Manchester University Press.

McKenzie, D. F. (1999) *Bibliography and the Sociology of Texts*, Cambridge: Cambridge University Press.

——(2002) *Making Meaning: 'Printers of the Mind' and other essays*, eds P. D. McDonald and M. F. Suarez, Amherst, MA: University of Massachusetts Press.

McLuhan, M. (1962) *The Gutenberg Galaxy: The making of typographic man*, London: Routledge & Kegan Paul.

MacRaild, D. M. and Taylor, A. (2004) *Social Theory and Social History*, Basingstoke, UK: Palgrave Macmillan.

Mandler, P. (2004) 'The Problem with Cultural History', *Cultural and Social History*, 1: 94–117.

Mandressi, R. (2003) *Le regard de l'anatomiste: dissections et invention du corps en Occident*, Paris: Seuil.

Martschukat, J. and Patzold, S. (eds) (2003) *Geschichtswissenschaft und 'performative turn': Ritual, Inszenierung und Performanz vom Mittelalter bis zur Neuzeit*, Cologne: Böhlau.

Marx, K. (1971) *A Contribution to the Critique of Political Economy*, ed. M. Dobb, London: Lawrence & Wishart.

Marx, K. and Engels, F. (1965) *The German Ideology*, London: Lawrence & Wishart [first published 1932].

Maurer, M. (2008) *Kulturgeschichte. Eine Einführung*, Cologne: Böhlau.

Mazour-Matusevich, Y. (2005) 'Writing Medieval History: An Interview with Aaron Gurevich', *Journal of Medieval and Early Modern Studies*, 35: 121–58.

Meade, T. A. and Wiesner-Hanks, M. E. (2004) *A Companion to Gender History*, Malden, MA/Oxford: Blackwell.

Ménétra, J.-L. (1986) *Journal of my Life*, ed. D. Roche, New York: Columbia University Press.

Mirzoeff, N. (ed.) (2006) *The Visual Culture Reader*, 2nd edn, London: Routledge.

Mitchell, W. J. T. (1994) *Picture Theory: Essays on verbal and visual representation*, Chicago, IL/London: University of Chicago Press.

——(2002) 'Showing Seeing: A critique of visual culture', *Journal of Visual Culture*, 1: 165–81.

——(2005a) 'There Are No Visual Media', *Journal of Visual Culture*, 4: 257–66.

——(2005b) *What Do Pictures Want? The lives and loves of images*, Chicago, IL: University of Chicago Press.

Morra, J. and Smith, M. (eds) (2006) *Visual Culture: Critical concepts in media and cultural studies*, four volumes, London: Routledge.

Muir, E. (2005) *Ritual in Early Modern Europe*, 2nd edn, Cambridge: Cambridge University Press.

Niccoli, O. (1979) *I sacerdoti, i guerrieri e i contadini: storia di un'immagine della società*, Turin: Einaudi.

Nora, P. (ed.) (1996–98) *Realms of Memory*, ed. L. B. Kritzman, trans. A. Goldhammer, three volumes, New York: Columbia University Press [partial trans. of work originally published 1984–92].

——(ed.) (2001–10) *Rethinking France = Les Lieux de mémoire*, trans. D. P. Jordan, four volumes, Chicago, IL/London: University of Chicago Press [partial trans. of work originally published 1984–92].

O'Brien, P. (1989) 'Michel Foucault's History of Culture', in L. Hunt (ed.) *The New Cultural History*, Berkeley, CA/London: University of California Press, pp. 25–46.

Orsi, P. L. (1983) 'La storia delle mentalità in Bloch e Febvre', *Rivista di storia contemporanea*, 12: 370–95.

Ory, P. (2004) *L'histoire culturelle*, Paris: PUF.

Pallares-Burke, M. L. (2002) *The New History: Confessions and conversations*, Oxford: Polity.

Panofsky, E. (1962) 'Artist, Scientist, Genius: Notes on the "Renaissance-Dämmerung"', in W. K. Ferguson, R. S. Lopez, G. Sarton, R. H. Bainton, L. Bradner and E. Panofsky, *The Renaissance: Six essays*, New York: Harper Torchbooks, pp. 121–82.

——(1991) *Perspective as Symbolic Form* [1927], New York: Zone.

Paterson, M. (2007) *The Senses of Touch: Haptics, affects, and technologies*, Oxford/New York: Berg.

Patlagean, E. (1988) 'L'histoire de l'imaginaire', in J. Le Goff (ed.) *La nouvelle histoire*, new edn, Brussels: Complexe, pp. 307–34.

Perry, M. (2002) *Marxism and History*, Basingstoke, UK: Palgrave Macmillan.

Pesez, L.-M. (1988) 'Histoire de la culture matérielle', in J. Le Goff (ed.) *La nouvelle histoire*, new edn, Brussels: Complexe, pp. 191–227.

Poirrier, P. (2004) *Les enjeux de l'histoire culturelle*, Paris: Seuil [repr. with addenda, 2010].

——(ed.) (2008) *L'Histoire culturelle: un 'tournant mondial' dans l'historiographie?*, postface R. Chartier, Dijon: Editions Universitaires de Dijon (Italian edn, co-ed. A. Arcangeli, *La storia culturale: una svolta nella storiografia mondiale?*, Verona: QuiEdit, 2010).

Porter, R. (2001) 'History of the Body Reconsidered', in P. Burke (ed.) *New Perspectives on Historical Writing*, 2nd edn, Cambridge: Polity, pp. 233–60.

Praz, M. (1970) *The Romantic Agony*, trans. A. Davidson, 2nd edn, London/ New York: Oxford University Press.

Prins, G. (2001) 'Oral History', in P. Burke (ed.) *New Perspectives on Historical Writing*, 2nd edn, Cambridge: Polity, pp. 120–56.

Prosperi, A. (1996) *Tribunali della coscienza*, Turin: Einaudi.

Ranke, L. von (2010) *On the Theory and Practice of History*, ed. G. G. Iggers, London: Routledge.

Reddy, W. M. (2001) *The Navigation of Feeling: A Framework for the History of Emotions*, Cambridge: Cambridge University Press.

Reeser, T. W. and Spaldin, S. D. (2002) 'Reading Literature/Culture: A Translation of "Reading as a Cultural Practice"', *Style*, 36: 659–76.

Revel, J. (1986a) 'Mentalités', in A. Burguière (ed.) *Dictionnaire des sciences historiques*, Paris: PUF, pp. 450–56.

——(1986b) 'Outillage mentale', in A. Burguière (ed.) *Dictionnaire des sciences historiques*, Paris: PUF, pp. 497–98.

Richardson, B. (1994) *Print Culture in Renaissance Italy: The editor and the vernacular text, 1470–1600*, Cambridge: Cambridge University Press.

——(2009) *Manuscript Culture in Renaissance Italy*, Cambridge: Cambridge University Press.

Ritter, J. and Gründer, K. (eds) (1971–2005) *Historisches Wörterbuch der Philosophie*, twelve volumes, Basel: Schwabe.

Roberts, G. (2001) *The History and Narrative Reader*, London: Routledge.

Roche, D. (1994) *The Culture of Clothing: Dress and fashion in the 'ancien regime'*, trans J. Birrell, Cambridge: Cambridge University Press.

——(2000) *A History of Everyday Things: The birth of consumption in France, 1600–1800*, trans. B. Pearce, Cambridge: Cambridge University Press.

——(2003) *Humeurs vagabondes: de la circulation des hommes et de l'utilité des voyages*, Paris: Fayard.

Rocke, M. (1996) *Forbidden Friendships: Homosexuality and male culture in Renaissance Florence*, New York/Oxford: Oxford University Press.

Rodríguez Gonzáles, A. L. (ed.) (2004) *Pensar la cultura: los nuevos retos de la historia cultural*, Medellín: Editorial Universidad de Antioquia.

Roodenburg, H. (2010) 'La terra di Huizinga: qualche appunto sulla storia culturale nei Paesi bassi', trans. A. Arcangeli, in P. Poirrier and A. Arcangeli (eds) *La storia culturale: una svolta nella storiografia mondiale?*, Verona: QuiEdit, pp. 183–201.

Rosenwein, B. H. (2002) 'Worrying about Emotions in History', *American Historical Review*, 107: 821–45.

——(2006) *Emotional Communities in the Early Middle Ages*, Ithaca, NY: Cornell University Press.

Rousselle, A. (1986) 'Corps', in A. Burguière (ed.) *Dictionnaire des sciences historiques*, Paris: PUF, pp. 156–61.

Rubin, M. (2002) 'What is Cultural History Now?', in D. Cannadine (ed.) *What Is History Now?*, Basingstoke, UK: Palgrave Macmillan, pp. 80–94.

Rublack, U. (2010) *Dressing Up: Cultural identity in Renaissance Europe*, Oxford: Oxford University Press.

Runciman, W. G. (2009) *The Theory of Cultural and Social Selection*, Cambridge: Cambridge University Press.

Rüsen, J. (ed.) (2002) *Western Historical Thinking: An intercultural debate*, New York/Oxford: Berghahn Books.

Saenger, P. (1997) *Space Between Words: The origins of silent reading*, Stanford, CA: Stanford University Press.

Salmi, H. (2008) *Nineteenth-century Europe: A cultural history*, Cambridge: Polity.

Sarti, R. (2004) *Vita di casa. Abitare, mangiare, vestire nell'Europa moderna*, 2nd edn, Rome/Bari: Laterza, www.laterza.it/vitadicasa.

Schama, S. (1995) *Landscape and Memory*, London: HarperCollins.

Schmitt, J.-C. (1990) *La raison des gestes dans l'Occident médiéval*, Paris: Gallimard.

Scott, J. W. (1988) *Gender and the Politics of History*, New York: Columbia Unversity Press.

——(1999) 'Some Reflections on Gender and Politics', in M. M. Ferree, J. Lorber and B. B. Hess (eds) *Revisioning Gender*, Thousand Oaks, CA/London: Sage, pp. 70–96.

——(2001) 'Women's History', in P. Burke (ed.) *New Perspectives on Historical Writing*, 2nd edn, Cambridge: Polity, pp. 43–70.

Scribner, R. W. (1994) *For the Sake of the Simple Folk: Popular propaganda for the German Reformation*, 2nd edn, Oxford: Oxford University Press.

Serna, J. and Pons, A. (2000) *Cómo se escribe la microhistoria*, Madrid: Cátedra Frónesis-Universitat de València.

——(2005) *La historia cultural: autores, obras, lugares*, Madrid: Akal.

Shapin, S. (1994) *A Social History of Truth: Civility and science in seventeenth-century England*, Chicago, IL/London: University of Chicago Press.

Shapin, S. and Schaffer, S. (1985) *Leviathan and the Air-Pump: Hobbes, Boyle, and the experimental life*, Princeton, NJ: Princeton University Press.

Sharpe, J. (2001) 'History from Below', in P. Burke (ed.) *New Perspectives on Historical Writing*, 2nd edn, Cambridge: Polity, pp. 25–42.

Sigurdson, R. (2004) *Jacob Burckhardt's Social and Political Thought*, Toronto/Buffalo/London: University of Toronto Press.

Smail, D. L. (2008) *On Deep History and the Brain*, Berkeley, CA/London: University of California Press.

Smith, M. (ed.) (2008) *Visual Culture Studies*, Los Angeles, CA/London: Sage.

Smith, M. M. (2007) *Sensory History*, Oxford: Berg.

Snowman, D. (2007) *Historians*, Basingstoke, UK: Palgrave Macmillan.

Spitzer, L. (1963) *Classical and Christian Ideas of World Harmony: Prolegomena to an interpretation of the word* Stimmung, Baltimore, MD: Johns Hopkins University Press.

Stearns, P. N. (1994) *American Cool: Constructing a twentieth-century emotional style*, New York/London: New York University Press.

Thomas, K. (1971) *Religion and the Decline of Magic: Studies in popular beliefs in sixteenth- and seventeenth-century England*, London: Weidenfeld & Nicolson.

——(1983) *Man and the Natural World: Changing attitudes in England, 1500–1800*, London: Allen Lane.

Thompson, E. P. (1991) *Customs in Common*, London: Merlin.

Tschopp, S. S. (2008) *Kulturgeschichte*, Stuttgart: Franz Steiner Verlag.

Tschopp, S. S. and Weber, W. (2006) *Grundfragen der Kulturgeschichte*, Darmstadt: WBG.

Valensi, L. and Wachtel, N. (1996) 'L'anthropologie historique', in J. Revel and N. Wachtel (eds) *Une école pour les sciences sociales*, Paris: Éditions du Cerf-Éditions de l'ÉHÉSS, pp. 251–74.

Viazzo, P. P. (2000) *Introduzione all'antropologia storica*, Rome/Bari: Laterza.

Viroli, M. (1998) *Machiavelli*, Oxford: Oxford University Press.

de Vivo, F. (2010) 'Prospect or Refuge? Microhistory, History on the Large Scale', *Cultural and Social History*, 7: 387–97.

Vovelle, M. (1990) *Ideologies and Mentalities*, trans. E. O'Flaherty, Cambridge: Polity.

Walker, J. A. and Chaplin, S. (1997) *Visual Culture: An introduction*, Manchester, UK: Manchester University Press.

Wehler, H.-U. (2001) *Historisches Denken am Ende des 20. Jahrhunderts: 1945–2000*, Göttingen: Wallstein.

Welch, E. (2005) *Shopping in the Renaissance*, New Haven, CT: Yale University Press.

Wesseling, H. (2001) 'Overseas History', in P. Burke (ed.) *New Perspectives on Historical Writing*, 2nd edn, Cambridge: Polity, pp. 71–96.

Whatmore, R. and Young, B. (2006) *Palgrave Advances in Intellectual History*, New York/Basingstoke, UK: Palgrave Macmillan.

White, H. (1973) *Metahistory: The historical imagination in nineteenth-century Europe*, Baltimore, MD: Johns Hopkins University Press.

Williams, R. (1958) *Culture and Society, 1780–1950*, New York: Columbia University Press.

Wunenburger, J.-J. (2003) *L'Imaginaire*, Paris: PUF.

Index

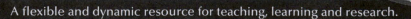